A GUIDE TO
METAL TOYS

A GUIDE TO
METAL TOYS

CONSTANCE KING

A QUINTET BOOK

Published in the USA 1996 by JG Press.
Distributed by World Publications, Inc.

The JG Press imprint is a trademark of
JG Press, Inc.
455 Somerset Avenue
North Dighton, MA 02764

This edition produced for sale in the USA, its
territories and dependencies only.

ISBN 1-57215-181-1

This book was designed and produced by
Quintet Publishing Limited
6 Blundell Street
London N7 9BH

Creative Director: Peter Bridgewater
Art Director: Ian Hunt
Designers: Stuart Walden, James Lawrence
Project Editor: Judith Simons
Editor: Robert Stewart
Picture Researcher: Jane Vandell Associates

Typeset in Great Britain by
QV Typesetting, London
Manufactured in Hong Kong by
Regent Publishing Services Limited
Printed in Singapore by
Star Standard Industries (Pte) Ltd

CONTENTS

INTRODUCTION

OYS, UNLIKE MANY other antiques, have an almost universal appeal. Everyone owned at least a few playthings in childhood and experienced the joy of acquisition that is very similar to the excitement the adult collector feels when buying a rare model car or an exceptionally fine French automaton. While a piece of jade or a Meissen dessert service would appeal to only a few people, antique toys arrest the attention of the urbane and the unsophisticated alike. Because of this high level of interest, prices have spiralled and collectors compete for especially good pieces.

In character, metal toy collectors range from the tough, mechanically minded, who quantify the rarity of trains or buy mint-condition, die-cast models to be hoarded away in their boxes, to those who only purchase toys that can be used as decorative antiques, and are inevitably attracted to automata, those exquisitely constructed mechanical figures that were originally made for display.

Each week, across Europe and the United States, there are busy shows, fairs and swap-meets, where enthusiasts can sort through a vast assortment of merchandise or sell their own surplus items. Most of the large salerooms now run regular auctions of toys and those auctions are often further divided into specialist areas such as soldiers, die-casts and tinplate toys. In most antique markets and centres there are a few toy dealers, though decorative pieces such as automata are also found in the stock of general dealers. In the United States and Australia, a number of specialists publish mail-order lists of their stock, so that collectors in the most remote places are constantly offered fresh items.

The most expensive toys are the automata, especially those made in France by such famous firms as Decamps, Lambert or Bontems, all of whom worked in Paris. These companies created tableaux and mechanized figures that imitated or parodied contemporary life, so that we find monkeys dressed in the costume of society elegants and beautiful bisque-headed ladies who preen themselves in dainty mirrors or appear to play the piano. Such figures are very expensive to produce and were made, not for children, but as luxury novelty gifts for adults. An automaton often took pride of place in the drawing room or boudoir and was set in motion as a special treat for visitors. Much simpler versions were

OPPOSITE *Made c 1902 by Gebrüder Bing of Nuremberg, this hand-painted model of the* Spider *car is one of the earliest pieces available to the collector of motor vehicles.*

RIGHT *A group of toys made by leading manufacturers: a battleship by Gebrüder Bing, c 1912; a clockwork '0' gauge Märklin engine, tender and rolling stock; and a boxed Britain's colour party.*

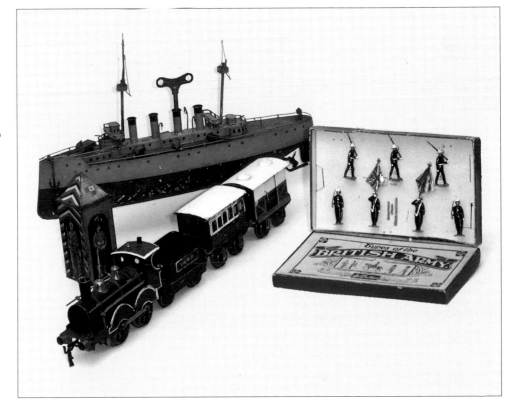

made as toys, such as babies that appear to cry when their prams are pulled along or birds that flap their wings and lay eggs; but even these can now be quite expensive.

Because of the inherent quality of automata there is little surprise when individual pieces sell for record prices; but when a tin toy sells for thousands, surprise is always expressed, since the objects were originally mass-produced and cheap. Tinplate toys emerged as a respectable collecting field in the 1960s and thereafter prices for the better pieces moved steadily upwards, though they have levelled off recently. The most popular items reflect contemporary transport, especially cars and delivery vehicles, and a well-preserved tourer by Carette or a spendid battleship (complete

with lifeboats) by the other great German firm, Bing, always finds an eager buyer. Such manufacturers produced good-quality models, heavily constructed to withstand years of play, and though the paintwork is often damaged, the basic toy frequently remains in working order.

Another German maker, Lehmann, created more amusing, but ephemeral, pieces, such as a clown attempting to control a wayward donkey or a bride battering her new husband — the type of piece that a pavement vendor could display to city gentlemen on the look-out for a colourful toy for a son or godchild. Lehmann clockwork toys were made from fairly thin, very brightly lithographed tinplate and they now offer an attractive collecting field, as a large number have

survived. Penny-toys were another popular line for street sellers — tiny models of horses, carriages, cars and trains. They now hold great appeal because so many of them can be displayed in a small space.

As early tinplate has become more expensive, people have turned in growing numbers to the more recent die-casts that were produced in much greater variety for the more affluent children of the post-war period. These accurate models, most highly valued when they are still in their original boxes, are now so tightly priced and categorized that collecting them has become as formal a business as collecting stamps or coins, with regular price lists and narrow classifications. So many have survived that it is easy to become hooked, and since they

can still occasionally be found in a jumble or garage sale, the chance of discovering a rarity is always just around the corner.

As early toys have become harder to find, a reproduction and 'collectors' edition' market has developed. Some of the firms which cater for that market do, indeed, reproduce the products they created many years ago; others issue limited editions of toys in a modern idiom, such as cars or London buses. As many of these toys sell cheaply, they offer to people who do not wish to spend a great deal of money the chance to become part of the collecting fraternity. On the other hand, limited editions, particularly die-casts, sometimes escalate rapidly in value, so that it is also possible, with a good eye, to buy as an investment.

In this book, the main collecting areas are discussed and advice is given on how to avoid expensive mistakes, how to care for old toys and how to spot the work of some of the most famous makers. When first produced, most toys were made for pleasure. Above all, collecting should be enjoyable, concerned not so much with investment as with the appreciation of a maker's artistry.

ABOVE *A page from a Nuremberg toy seller's catalogue, dated to 1877, shows the immense variety of tin toys produced during this period. Particularly interesting are the trains, which, like some of the toys depicted on other pages of the catalogue, are very retrospective.*

RIGHT *An early live-steam, spirit-fired battleship, the King Edward, made by Gebrüder Bing of Nuremberg c 1902. This large-scale model has a wealth of detail, including ship's boats and five cannon. The gilded bow decoration is typical of the period.*

AUTOMATA

ANY TOY ENTHUSIASTS like to describe the items they collect as works of art, but it is in the area of automata that the term is most justified. The finest of these creations, ones that imitated the movements of people and animals, were individually made to the highest standard as exhibition pieces and they are such rare objects that they are almost impossible to value. In the areas of top-quality automata, mass-production techniques had no place; each figure was meticulously decorated and costumed for a most discerning market: that of the adult rather than the child.

The golden age of automata was the late 19th century, when French, German and Swiss makers exported a galaxy of colourful figures and tableaux all over the world. German clockmakers, in the early Renaissance, created the first commercial mechanical children's toys combining music and some form of movement. As Germany developed as the toy-making centre of the world, movement was given to doll and animal figures produced cheaply for the infant market. Some of the figures with bisque heads, mounted on paper-covered musical boxes, and still sold in the 1920s, are very similar to those made in the 18th century, as the manufacturers preferred well-tried, economical designs.

French makers concentrated on the luxury trade and delighted in complicated mechanisms and extravagant clothes and accessories. Sometimes the small fan that a fashionable lady is holding is so exquisitely painted that it could find a place in a collection of miniatures, while even the shoe-buckles and gloves are exact copies, finished with an attention to detail that is not found on clothes made for automata in any other country.

The finest automata were made in and around Paris mainly during the latter half of the 19th century, where manufacturers such as Théroude, Decamps, Lambert and Vichy relied on the creative skills of hundreds of outworkers, who produced the costumes and accessories. Swiss musical movements were often used by the French makers, as their quality was exceptionally high, and German dolls' heads were also utilized, so that a single automaton frequently incorporates parts from all three countries.

OPPOSITE *This piano-playing automaton, with a bisque head made by Emile Jumeau, turns and nods her head as she 'plays' with three movements. The 4½-inch cylinder plays four airs which are listed on the tune sheet on the piano. French; maker unknown.*

LEFT *An extremely rare clockwork coach of gilt metal, made by the English maker William Nightingale in 1766. The horses appear to gallop when the clockwork mechanism, concealed beneath the seat, is activated. A metal plaque carries the maker's name and the date of manufacture. 10½ inches long.*

THE PRE-MODERN ERA

REPRESENTATIONS OF OBJECTS that appear to live and move have appealed to people through the centuries. The Greeks used articulated statues to answer questions and perform in miraculous ways, usually with the assistance of a small man or boy concealed in the base. The greatest advances were made by Hero of Alexandria (285-222 BC). His writings and diagrams reveal complex machines that made figures turn and move by means of hydraulic and pneumatic power. Among his automata were a figure of Hercules who shot an arrow at a hissing dragon lying under a tree and another of singing birds that were operated by water pressure.

In medieval Europe, Bernadino Baldi also created automata that worked by a hydraulic system and there are references to mechanical animals and figures that were seen at various courts. The development of the commercial automaton began with the 16th-century clockmakers, who included central figures such as Death striking the hours or the Adoration of the Magi. Augsburg and Nuremberg were the first important centres of this mechanical art, examples of which have survived in some churches and public buildings. Small table clocks with articulated scenes from Italian comedy or classical mythology were also made in Germany. The skill of the Nuremberg craftsmen in creating flying and moving creatures was revered and their workshops were the source of many princely gifts.

THE 18TH-CENTURY MASTERS

AUTOMATA MANUFACTURE HAD become a specialized art form by the 18th century and was already divided into two sections, one for children and the other for wealthy adults, who appreciated the complexity of the latest novelty. Tableaux such as

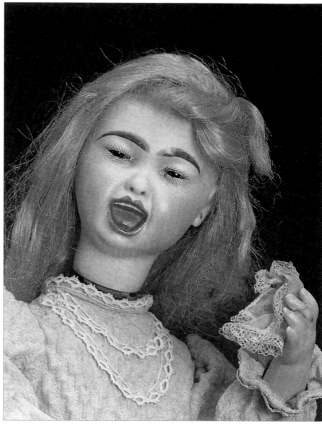

game hunts, a blacksmith's shop or a coach and horses that moved around a cabinet give some indication of the luxury pieces that could be purchased in exclusive shops. The curiosity of the general public was satisfied by exhibitions, where specially constructed display pieces, such as a six-ft (two-m) figure that played the flute when air was forced through his mouth, could be viewed.

Jacques de Vaucanson (1907-82) was the most famous early-18th-century maker. His automata included a gilded copper duck that drank, ate, splashed about in water and then digested its food, presumably with the aid of chemicals. Other figures made by him for public display were worked by weights, cams and levers; these included a figure that could play 11 melodies on a flute. Such figures exploited some of the most advanced mechanical skills of the period and it is not surprising that Vaucanson, bored with creating novelties, should have sold his automata to a travelling showman and turned his attention to more serious scientific work.

Sadly, Vaucanson's creations are all lost. But his work was

carried on by a Swiss clockmaker, Pierre Jaquet-Droz (1721-90). The most famous figures that he made can still be seen performing at the waterside museum in Neuchâtel, Switzerland. Pierre and Henri Louis Jaquet-Droz and Jean Frédéric Leschot (1746-1827) made figures that were more realistic than anything previously attempted and it is little wonder that they were exhibited all over Europe, together with a charming country scene that contained a number of animated characters.

Pierre Jaquet-Droz had run a very successful clockmaking business before he decided, after a nervous breakdown, to create automata. They were more lifelike than anything previously attempted. He finished a boy draughtsman and, in collaboration with Leschot, a writer in 1773 — figures that were to make his firm famous throughout Europe. *The Writer*, representing a boy about three years old seated at a table, is believed to have been constructed by Pierre. The mechanism is extremely intricate because so many moving parts had to be fitted inside a child-size body. As the boy writes, with a goose-quill pen, his eyes turn to follow the words in a realistic manner. The complex mechanism allows the boy to write sentences that contain a maximum of 40 letters. The problems that collectors face in caring for the mechanisms of fine automata is highlighted by *The Writer*: if the temperature drops too suddenly, he is liable to make spelling mistakes and space his words unevenly.

The *Little Draughtsman* and *The Writer* were put on display at all the European courts and centres of fashion. In order to flatter Louis XV of France the *Little Draughtsman* drew a delicate portrait of him, copies of which can still be purchased at Neuchâtel. The *Draughtsman* is completely different in construction to *The Writer*. The paper on which he draws remains stationary. Three interchangeable sets of cams, each having twelve cams, enable the boy to make four drawings and a system of bellows enables him to blow the dust off his paper with great realism. This automaton was made over a

two-year period and is now visited by every automata enthusiast, who can study the detail of the mechanism in films and diagrams.

A third figure, the *Lady Musician*, is so complex and functional that her mechanism is often studied by makers of robots. She is much larger than the boys and her fingers move individually, so that she actually plays the instrument by means of a complicated system of rods and levers. Such complexity of movement was rarely attempted, as the cost was prohibitive, but it was the ideal that all later craftsmen attempted to imitate more economically. As the *Musician* plays, her breast rises and falls, a relatively uncomplicated movement that is seen in a number of later, more doll-like, figures. When the lady pauses in her play, she turns her head, moves her eyes, glances down modestly and then up again, bends forward and straightens up. On the completion of each melody she brings a fourth mechanism into action, which enables her to bow graciously as if acknowledging the audience's approval.

LEFT *A group of French automata.* FROM LEFT TO RIGHT· *The Negro Flautist by Vichy, c 1880; he raises his head, blinks, moves his lower jaw and 'plays' the flute with articulated fingers. A Leopold Lambert Butterfly Catcher, c 1880, nods her head as she endeavours to catch the insect. The Vichy musical Oriental Woman is selling Japanese Noh masks; the composition-headed figure raises one mask while her umbrella twirls, her head turns and her eyes blink. The musical Girl with a Hoop was made by Leopold Lambert; her head turns as her arms move the sticks. The musical Monkey Banjo Player, made by Vichy c 1880, blinks and bares his teeth, and turns and nods his head to music as he strums with his right hand.*

OPPOSITE *The Autoperipatetikos was produced with a variety of different heads and costumes. This porcelain-headed lady has the skirt lifted to show the cardboard cone that conceals the mechanism. It was patented by Enoch Rice Morrison on 15 July, 1862.*

These three Neuchâtel figures represent the peak of automata manufacture and mark the beginning of the modern development of the art; other figures are always judged against them. The problems that this trio have posed to the restorers are the same as those faced by collectors, who have to make decisions about re-costuming, re-painting and replacing damaged parts. Like many lesser automata, they suffered badly in the hands of several owners, who considered them purely as amusing spectacles. Not until the early 20th century was the importance of their mechanisms fully appreciated and a painstaking programme of restoration and conservation begun.

Jaquet-Droz was especially concerned with complex hand movements; commercial toy manufacturers were more interested in making a figure appear to walk by placing one foot in front of the other. Doll-like toys that moved forward by means of wheels concealed under a skirt had been made since the Renaissance, but Charles Abram Bruguier (1788-1862) is

clashing cymbals or hammering some item on a work-bench.

One of the few British makers whose work has survived is John Hempel, who signed his somewhat crudely made display pieces on the base. His figures were sold by Edlins Rational Repository of Amusement and Instruction, whose rectangular labels are also found on the underside of scenes such as 'the snuff taker', 'spinning' or 'the influenza sufferer'. These automata, with plaster heads and a wooden body framework articulated by a series of leather hinges and wire springs, are quite primitive, but they are frequently included in collections as the first available commercial products. Somewhat similar figures combining music and figures that are ironing or spinning were made in France and they attract interest if in good condition.

The *Silver Swan*, exhibited at Barnard Castle in County Durham, England, gives some idea of the quality and elegance that was achieved in the 18th century. The life-sized swan preens itself and then gives the illusion of catching a fish from the surrounding water. Originally, the swan was accompanied by a canopy of mirrors, which added sparkle and glamour to the scene, but these were lost in the Victorian period. The swan was first exhibited by James Cox (d 1788), a London watchmaker who ran a museum of automata that contained more than 50 exhibits. At that time, the leading clock and automata manufacturers sold their products to a limited, very wealthy, clientele and they were already combining their skills to take advantage of the international market. After James Cox died — his son combined with Jaques-Droz and Henri Maillardet (b 1745) — his automata were dispersed across the world, from Russia to China, where they were exhibited at the courts.

THE GOLDEN ERA: 19TH-CENTURY FRENCH MASTERS

THOUGH COLLECTORS LIKE to own a few examples of early automata, the majority are mainly interested in pieces made after 1860, when commercial production began in earnest. The rich European merchant classes, eager to find new and eye-catching gifts, offered the makers a ready and ever-expanding market. As Paris was the centre of international

believed to have been the first to make a doll, introduced in 1821, with a more realistic walking mechanism. At that time commercial automata, made for sale in toy and gift shops, were relatively simple, and when they come on the market, they often sell for less, despite their early date, than later, but more complex, figures. Their simple mechanisms are usually concealed in a flat, box-like base on which the hand-wound figures perform basic movements, such as beating a drum,

ABOVE *A Gustave Vichy Musical Dunce, c 1890. The figure, seated on a table containing a key-wound, stop-start mechanism, kicks his leg, shakes his donkey ears and lifts his right arm.*

ABOVE RIGHT *The Bread Seller made by Leopold Lambert, with a Jumeau bisque head, c 1885. This automaton plays one air as the figure offers a loaf of bread while nodding and turning its head.*

OPPOSITE *A Leopold Lambert automaton with a bisque Jumeau head. The girl turns and nods as she raises and lowers the strings of the toy Polichinelle, which has a composition head.*

fashion, with a whole variety of beautiful luxury items produced by small, exclusive manufacturers, it was inevitable that the most beautiful and highly refined automata should be made there.

Automata that represented beautiful children and women were difficult to produce if the heads had to be made of *papier mâché* or painted wood, but from 1855 French and German porcelain factories began to manufacture dolls' heads of great delicacy and elegance. The availability of these attractive bisque heads seems to have inspired the makers to create a procession of finely costumed ladies and large-eyed beautiful children and they continue to delight their owners. Court ladies fan themselves or powder their noses; children play the piano or chase a butterfly; a nurse pushes a pretty baby in a perambulator; or circus and stage characters perform their antics to a musical accompaniment.

Many of the French automata contain Swiss musical movements which were mass-produced from the 1870s. The first means of reproducing music mechanically had been the

barrel organ, but the musical box was much more adaptable
and was invented in 1796 as a novelty for snuff-boxes. In the
early 19th century, Geneva was the international centre of
the trade, though the larger sizes were usually made at Ste
Croix. With dolls' heads and musical movements available,
together with an army of skilled outworkers who could create
ravishing costumes from scraps of tinsel, silk and lace, a
galaxy of automata was ready to move on stage. As the heads
remained in pristine condition, these figures are still as lovely
today as when they were first created.

In contrast to the sophistication of the faces, the bodies of
automata are surprisingly crude; parts that were to be con-

cealed by the costume were neither decorated nor well finished. As most of the figures were made to order in very limited numbers, there was no reason to use mass-production methods, such as those used for making the bodies of play dolls. Instead, the makers worked more in the manner of artists, and created simple moulds into which sheets of carton spread with glue could be pressed. On some bodies the individual layers of carton are obvious; in others, especially those intended as children's toys, a composition substance which gave a smoother effect was used. If the legs and arms were to be revealed, a more refined composition was necessary and any joins were well sanded before flesh-coloured paint was

applied. Sometimes, especially on figures of ladies, porcelain or bisque lower arms or hands gave a more delicate effect. In many instances, bisque heads were used in combination with composition hands, a mixture of materials which sometimes makes new collectors suspicious.

To sophisticated automata enthusiasts, the interest of the figure depends more on the complexity of the movement than on the beauty of the head. When the automaton is small, but contains a large number of cams and levers for several movements, the great skill of the manufacturer is especially apparent. Sometimes the musical movement is contained in the figure or hidden beneath a chair or a table, again evidence

of the skill of the designer. In cheaper, more commercial, examples, the musical box is fitted in the base, which can be covered with velvet or imaginatively disguised as a rock, a tower or a moss-covered bank.

As most automata play only one or two airs, those with a larger number are especially valuable, especially if the musical box itself is of high quality. As the figures and pieces of scenery were mounted in different ways, the same doll might appear in combination with musical boxes of varying quality, so that it is necessary to become very familiar with a piece before any valuation is attempted.

The French makers of automata worked to the demand of their customers and, as their products were always expensive, they often made only 10 or 20 of a particular model. Little wonder, then, that some figures are extremely rare and command very high prices. All makers produced some of their simpler, more economical, figures and groups in larger, more commercial, numbers. Leopold Lambert, in particular, produced some of his doll-like figures again and again, but since he used very pretty dolls' heads, usually made by Jumeau, his less rare automata sell for good prices.

An automaton by Leopold Lambert is usually one of the first purchases of the new enthusiast. The firm specialized in mechanical figures of a doll-like nature with bisque heads made by the leading makers. Lambert had originally worked for the respected firm of Vichy, in whose workrooms he learned many of the methods of making figures appear to smoke or blow bubbles. Most of the child-like figures he created stand on bases that contain the musical movement and they perform fairly basic actions, such as lifting the lid off a basket to show a bleating lamb or a singing bird. The simple cylinder musical movement usually plays only one air. His products are marked 'L.B.' on the keys. The firm also made some very complex and rare automata which are among the most expensive. One of the best-known figures is a smoker which inhales and blows out smoke. The bubble blower, with a bellows in the base connected to a tube at the mouth, is much rarer and less likely to be in working order if it is bought at auction.

A much wider range of automata was created by Vichy, a firm that was founded in *c* 1860 by Antoine Michel, Henry and Gustave Pierre Vichy. In general, the Vichy products are much more artistic than Lambert's and the heads, usually of

OPPOSITE *The musical* Pumpkin Eater *by Gustave Vichy, c 1870, has a papier-mâché head and forearms. A section of the pumpkin opens to reveal a mouse.*

ABOVE *A Decamps musical* Lute Player, *with bisque head and forearms, made c 1870. The figure's right hand plays the strings and he moves his head from side to side and nods. The musical mechanism is contained in the base.*

LEFT *A* Smoker *made by Decamps c 1870. The Jumeau shellacked bisque head has an open mouth; he lifts a bone cheroot with his right arm and pulls smoke through a tube in his arm and out through his mouth.*

BELOW *A musical Mexican Guitar Player made by Leopold Lambert c 1885. The figure has a papier-mâché head which moves from side to side and nods. His jaw drops to show a row of teeth. The base contains a key-wound, stop-start mechanism which plays two airs.*

ABOVE *A rare 25-key monkey duo organ, made in France during the late 19th century. It plays nine tunes on pipes mounted below the bellows. The winding handle is at the back and the tune-changing knife at the side. The monkey cello player has five movements and the violin player has six.*

OPPOSITE *A Roullet et Decamps Pierrot and the Moon. The tongue of the moon rolls from side to side. The Pierrot lifts one leg and his left arm as if to play a guitar. The key-wound mechanism is contained in the moon and plays a waltz.*

papier mâché, have more character, as they were specially made for the various subjects. The 'man in the moon' was often portrayed. One version shows a small clown seated on top of a full moon that pokes out its tongue and rolls its eyes, another a crescent moon, whose eyes roll as a clown, seated at the base and playing a guitar.

The stage and the circus provided all the makers of automata with a variety of subjects and Vichy was especially fascinated by the artistic potential of clowns and pierrots. One of the firm's more striking figures shows a pierrot seated at a writing table. His head turns to follow the pen as it moves across the page, but sleep is overcoming him and his eyes close and the light in the lamp dims. Awakening, he reaches to turn up the lamp and begins to write again. Another wistful pierrot, again with a *papier-mâché* head, is a hunchback who tempts a monkey perched on his shoulder with sugar.

Vichy acrobats perform delicately on the backs of chairs or on ladders, moving their weight from the right to the left hand before completing their act. Sometimes a monkey performs tricks or plays a banjo as he blinks and bares his teeth. Characters from many countries were represented in *papier mâché*, some of the negro fruit sellers standing 30in (75cm) high. A Japanese girl with a tray, an African lady sitting on a stool and playing a lyre, and even Buffalo Bill, made in *c* 1880, all came from the busy French maker.

Though not the most artistic of Vichy products, the *Magic Cupboard* is one of the pieces that every collector dreams of possessing. A naughty boy is seen sitting on a wooden buffet. He turns and reaches towards an upper door which opens. A fly then appears, but moves out of his reach. In the open cupboard he sees his goal, a pot of his grandmother's jam. He reaches for it, but it spins around to reveal his grandmother's face, her mouth opening and closing as she scolds him. He nods his head, gestures with his right hand and sticks out his tongue as the cupboard door closes. As though Vichy had not sufficiently proved its skill, a mouse then runs up the back of a cheese on the serving area. This very complex automaton is similar in style to some of the penny-in-the-slot machines that were also made by the firm, such as a pair of naughty boys who have been kept in at school. In 1905 Vichy was taken over by Triboulet and in 1923 it became part of the Société Jouets Automates Français.

In contrast to the sophisticated automata made by Vichy

for an adult market are the much more toy-like versions produced by Alexandre Nicolas Théroude. Between 1845 and 1872, Théroude registered 20 patents that related to automated animals, groups of musicians and various dolls. Collectors are most familiar with the dolls that come frequently on the market. They are marked on the base. The first patent (1845) was for a life-sized rabbit that moved its feet, ears and mouth before lifting its tail and dropping chocolates on the ground. Known as *Le Lapin Mal Elevé,* the toy also carried a sugar carrot.

A later patent described a hen, covered with feathers, that laid gilded wooden eggs. Théroude's fascination with animals was also shown in a series of life-sized goats and sheep which made his factory famous. By 1850 Théroude was described as a specialist maker of automata and toys and the inventor of a talking baby in a cradle. As he was, above all, a toymaker, many of his products were inexpensive items intended for the nursery. His dolls with *papier-mâché* heads were relatively simple, though some had turning heads, opening and closing eyes and arms that lifted to throw a kiss or smell a flower. Most moved on a wheeled mechanism and some were made more complicated after 1854, when Théroude developed a device for making a doll play the game 'cuckoo', during which it lifted its apron over its eyes. This toy carries the firm's mark on the metal mechanism.

Théroude's figures, such as monkeys playing violins or rabbits stroking their whiskers, often appeal more to toy collectors than automata specialists, who prefer the sophistication of drawing-room pieces such as those made by J. Phalibois. This firm, working from 22 Rue Charlot in Paris, specialized in complex mechanical groups arranged under glass shades. The quality of the automata is often reflected in their bases, the finest of which have an inlay of brass, mother-of-pearl or ivory. Some of these prestige items play as many as six airs, though the majority play only two. The musical movement is occasionally marked 'J. Phalibois' or the initials 'J.P.' are incised. Such marks are sometimes difficult to find, as they can be seen only when the mechanism is revealed.

Phalibois' favourite subject was the satin-costumed monkey, who is seen painting at an easel, nursing a baby, mending shoes or performing conjuring tricks. One automaton of a monkey artist was stamped inside the base, 'J. Phalibois, 22 Rue Charlot, Paris. F'gue Pièces Mécaniques, Fantasies à Musiques'. The maker, Durand & Jacob, was also associated and scenes that were created by Phalibois sometimes have keys marked 'D.J.'. Such associations of makers, combined with the occasional pirating of designs, often makes the attribution of unmarked automata very difficult, so that many are cautiously described as 'Phalibois type'.

Some of the groups under domes are 30in (75cm) high. They were intended as important pieces to be set in motion for visitors or to amuse children as a special treat. Scenes of a lady at a dressing table, stitching at her sewing machine or playing a piano were made with a flair for detail that is unmistakably French. One exceptionally decorative scene shows a tightrope walker carrying a flag in each hand. A negro and a Chinese musician stand on either side, the richness of their costumes reflected in the mirrored glass panels. The musical movement, incised 'J. Phalibois', plays four airs.

Occasionally the maker's name will be found on the glass shade, together with details of medals awarded at the various international exhibitions. Decamps, the most prolific maker

ABOVE A Monkey Fiddler *musical clock automaton, possibly made by Bontems. The figure has a papiermâché head and glass eyes. Hummingbirds are perched in the branches, and the scene even features a 'waterfall'.*

LEFT A Gustave Vichy Smoking Monkey, c 1860, *holds a lorgnette in one hand and an ivory cheroot holder in the other.*

OPPOSITE A Monkey Trio, *possibly made by Phalibois c 1870. The pull-string musical movement plays two interchangeable airs. The string players move their right arms and the harpist both its arms.*

Breton peasants wearing clogs with their satin, 18th-century-style dress. Domestic work was also idealized and there are exquisitely costumed washerwomen and ladies ironing in charming, but improbable, costumes. In the more interesting automata the musical movements are concealed in the torso or beneath a chair, as in the *Peasant with a Piglet.*

Not only French bisque and *papier-mâché* heads, but German bisque, composition and celluloid heads, were used by Decamps who, over a long period of manufacture, created knitters, a number of clowns, figures dancing on the moon and magicians that perform the cup-and-ball trick. One of the most alluring figures is the *Snake Dance*, believed to have originally represented Loïe Fuller, who performed at the Folies-Bergère. Many versions of this lady were made and they are usually dated by the style of the costume. Some of the doll-like figures, which perform simpler actions, have bisque heads made by Jumeau. Among them is the charming *Flower Seller.* This lady turns her head and gestures to a rose in her basket, which opens to reveal a small doll that throws a kiss.

The fantasy world of Decamps included a large number of animals: rabbits that emerge from tree trunks or cabbages, naughty dogs and cats, elephants, tigers and lions. The *Puss in Boots* automaton is always a favourite, as are some of the bears that are covered with rabbit fur and have moving jaws and front legs. Some of the bears play drums, others drink or smoke. As the bears are not rare, they are among the least expensive of the Decamps automata. So are some of the more toy-like figures, such as babies and animals that emerge from flowers or baskets.

After 1906, electricity was sometimes used instead of traditional clockwork mechanisms, allowing the creation of even more complex tableaux and window-display pieces. Decamps now produces a variety of figures using the most up-to-date technology. Sadly, even the luxury trade now finds such work too expensive, so that the finest modern automata have become the province of show business and the advertising world. One of the most complex figures made in recent years was created for the *Tales of Hoffmann* when it was performed at the Paris Opéra. This automaton, operated by remote control, walked, sang and danced on the stage each night and then fell to pieces.

The manufacture of window-display pieces was important until the 1930s, when shopkeepers seem to have lost interest

of automata, sometimes presented scenes such as *The Illusionist* in this way, a refinement that adds much to the collectable value of the piece. This firm, still in existence today, was established by Jean Roullet (1832-1907), originally a maker of mechanical toys, in the 1860s. After Roullet was joined by his son-in-law, Ernest Decamps (1847-1909), the firm manufactured shop-window display pieces as well as drawing-room automata. Though the Victorian work was good, some of the most complex pieces were made in the early 20th century, when the founder's grandsons ran the firm.

Some concept of the variety of automata made by Roullet et Decamps is provided in the pages of a 1912 catalogue, which illustrates male and female clowns, Mexican men, Arab girls, Japanese ladies fanning themselves and magicians who perform conjuring tricks, all, of course, costumed in rich satins trimmed with braid and sequins. The idealized life of country people has always appealed to French artists and we find silk-dressed peasants carrying a piglet that moves its head, shepherds in court dress serenading the birds, and in this method of attracting custom. Alongside the complex figures made by firms such as Decamps there were many basic structures that performed only one or two actions, such as lifting an arm or nodding the head. As no great skill was required for the manufacture of such pieces, especially after the advent of electricity, negro minstrels, nodding Chinamen and dwarfs, shoemakers and cheerful Father Christmas figures were made in every country. They were rarely marked by the maker, but the country of origin is sometimes stamped or embossed under the base. Such figures offer an attractive collecting area for those who do not want to spend too much money and yet want to create an unusual collection that is of period interest.

BEYOND FRANCE

THOUGH GREAT BRITAIN was never a producer of luxury automata, there are some very fine advertising and window-display figures, some of the rarest pieces being made by William Britain, who is more commonly associated with toy soldiers. These figures were strongly made, with lead heads, hands and legs. They are activated by clockwork. Somewhat smaller than many display automata, measuring under 17in (42cm), the figures have the maker's label fixed under the base. One figure, representing a Scotsman, pours whisky into a glass and appears to drink. He performs for half an hour at each winding, as did a Mandarin who drank tea. Such figures were expensive in relation to the toys sold by Britain and they were mainly intended as trade pieces. The clockwork *Khedive*, who could smoke cigarettes or a pipe and blew out clouds of smoke, was suggested as a novelty for a Christmas party, as was their *Indian Juggler*, a much larger toy than the *Khedive*. He taps a basket in front of him and raises the lid to show a child. He replaces the lid and lifts it again to reveal a snake. Automated collecting boxes for charity were also made by the firm, any of whose products are of great interest, as so few automated figures were made in Great Britain.

Superb coin-operated display automata were a speciality of Swiss makers, especially those based in Ste Croix. One of the most famous makers, Auguste Lassueur, entered into an agreement with a Swiss railway company in 1897 that allowed him to place his work in all waiting rooms. After the Swiss Federal Railways took over in 1938, these machines

were electrified and many of them can still be seen in operation. Typical of Lassueur's work are groups of dancing dolls on stages backed with mirrors, though the roundabouts with dolls sitting in boats and on horses are more lively. These coin-operated automata can play as many as six airs and they are collected by mechanical music enthusiasts as well as automata collectors.

Some interesting, but primitive, versions without musical movements were produced in Great Britain by William Tansley in the late 19th century. Using commercial dolls and horses, he created scenes at the races, performing minstrels and fairground dioramas with doors that open to reveal any-

ABOVE *A Vichy/Tribailet Monkey Piano Player. The musical movement, contained in the base, plays two airs and the figure's jaws, eyelids, head and arms move.*

OPPOSITE *A musical Monkey Artist, probably by Blaise Bontems c 1870. Six movements activate the eyes, jaw, head and the three actions of the painting arm. The bell striking clock by Lapy Frères has a Broco escapement.*

thing from marching soldiers to bellringers. Pieces by known makers always attract interest, but any fairground amusement machine with an especially well-made or amusing tableau will find a ready buyer. Such items are on the borderline between amusement machines and automata and are in general more attractive to collectors of fairground art.

Colourful coin-in-the-slot automata and window-display pieces were made in the United States, though never to the standard of the exclusive luxury products of France. In the mid-19th century, wealthy Americans relied on imported luxury goods from France and Germany. Though several firms were set up in America by immigrant craftsmen, there seems to have been no serious attempt to create automata to rival the French luxury products that were sold in the most exclusive stores. Instead, American manufacturers concentrated on the simpler automata that would appeal to children and be strong enough to withstand transportation to all parts of the country without damage. One of the most imaginative mid-19th-century makers was George W. Brown, who

ABOVE *A Gustave Vichy musical Acrobat, made c 1876. The figure balances on a gently swaying ladder with both hands, nodding his head and arching his back before levitating sideways on one hand. The musical movement plays two airs.*

worked at Forestville in Connecticut, a centre of the clock-making industry. Brown himself was a clockmaker by trade and was obviously interested in mechanized figures, regis-tering several patents for walking dolls.

Edward R. Ives, who also worked in Connecticut, is a much more important figure to collectors of automata. Though intended mainly for children, some of his figures are so beau-tifully made and dressed in such fine fabric that they hold their own against more sophisticated European products. Ives originally made toys that were activated by hot air, but by the 1880s a range of charming metal toys, such as a costumed lady driving a hippodrome chariot, was being made. The window-display figures, typical of the strong toys which Ives created, could run for long periods without re-winding.

Ives increased his range of automated toys after taking over a small New York maker, Robert J. Clay, who specialized in figures such as fur-covered bears, negro preachers and crawling babies. Ives also used the talent of Jerome Secor, who made singing birds in cages and metal-headed dolls per-

ABOVE *The papier-mâché headed gentleman lifts his arms as he moves along. He is one of various characters produced by Théroude and stands on the usual three-wheeled base.*

OPPOSITE *A Lutz-type, tinplate, one-horse sleigh made in Germany in the 1870s. The mechanism causes the horse to dip realistically as its moves forward. The figures are made of plaster and have a 'fur' rug to cover them. The horse is made of carved wood.*

forming such actions as playing the piano. Most famous of all the Ives' products are the stiff figures that 'walk' on wheels concealed under their large feet. Father Christmas, figures of various nationalities, Uncle Tom and General Benjamin Franklin Butler all marched out of the Ives factories costumed in fabric outfits. They were highly popular toys and examples frequently appear in the specialist salerooms.

An even more common American toy is the *Autoperipatetikos*, a doll that appeared to walk without support. It was patented by Enoch Rice Morrison in 1862. The dolls moved forwards by a key-wound clockwork mechanism that operated the feet independently, so that the figure took actual steps forward on rollers concealed under the metal boots. Large numbers of these toys were produced, all with the characteristic thick body that was necessary to conceal the mechanism. The commonest figure of this type is a lady in a crinoline dress, a toy whose value depends on the type of head used and the quality of the costume. Bisque, *papier mâché* and porcelain shoulder heads were used by the assemblers of the *Autoperipatetikos*, though the portrait figures representing people such as Napoleon III were made of composition with moulded beards.

The easily recognizable *Autoperipatetikos* was the first mass-produced doll to move forward with individual steps and an American inventor also designed the first talking figure to be manufactured in large numbers. Thomas Edison (1847-1931) marketed his first talking doll in 1889. It had a steel torso that contained a phonograph. The doll, with jointed limbs and a German bisque head, was wound from the back and recited a number of nursery rhymes and short sentences. These dolls were the first in a long series of talking figures made in every country and incorporating the most up-to-date technology. Each year, at the international toy trade fairs, yet another talking doll is launched. Yet, despite advances in technology, the sound of the voice is more unreal than in Edison's day. The ultimate realistic talking doll that can be mass-produced still eludes the toymakers.

Because German manufacturers were always more interested in the large-scale production of children's toys rather than individually made luxury items, their automata, like most British and American examples, are of the most basic kind. The majority of them perform simple actions such as lifting their arms and turning their heads, movements that are controlled by wires or cords. Costumed clockwork figures, such as those made by Ives in America, were not made by the German tin-toy makers. Simple automata became a speciality of the town of Sonneberg, especially famed for its production of dolls.

Activated German toys of the 1830s relied on two methods: a squeeze box with an animal or figure fixed to the sloping surface or a simple mechanism concealed in a box with a small crank at the side which set figures and, sometimes, music in motion. The tableaux arranged on hand-cranked boxes are particularly charming: soldiers who come to attention, a pair of fighting goats, a fox chasing a squirrel, and women taking sheep to market. A few of the toys represent contemporary life too truthfully for comfort: a butcher brings a chopper down on a bullock's neck, a man beats his donkey and a hunter kills a hare. Some of the box-like bases were painted with bright flowers, but more frequently they

were decorated with paper. Some idea of the vast range of figures sold in the early 19th century can be gained from the hand-coloured sample books of merchants such as J.S. Lindner of Sonneberg.

The most expensive versions of these early German toys have dolls with *papier-mâché* heads, dressed in fashionable gauze or muslin frocks with high waists and low necklines and playing musical instruments. One elegant gentleman is seated at an organ; another plays a violin with a jerky, simple movement. These hand-cranked scenes were brightly coloured and form an interesting commentary on the daily life of the period. Soldiers fired guns and cannon, street musicians have small monkeys as an added attraction, and monks, woodcutters, market traders and farm workers, blacksmiths and stonemasons all perform their daily tasks in the most basic way.

Circus and fairground life has provided automata makers of all countries with a constant source of inspiration and the workers of Sonneberg created tightrope walkers, conjurers, trapeze artists and clowns galore riding goats along with pigs and donkeys. Some of these early activated toys are complete scenes, with a backdrop against which elephants and giraffes parade with their keepers and ladies water their flower gardens or drink coffee in a sitting room. A few are virtual boxes with a roof, in which the figures perform in an enclosed, magical world of their own.

As the scenes and figures were made from composition, thin wood, wire, string and scraps of fabric and paper, they are extremely fragile. Few have survived in pristine condition. When they come on the market, they are bought both by toy and automata collectors, as they are among the most imaginative and well-made commercial figures ever produced. Variations on the types of figures marketed by Lindner continued to be produced throughout the 19th century. They are dated by the materials used and, especially, by the costumes. Squeaking, barking, tinkling and rattling, these toys performed in the nurseries in Europe and the United States and they can now be found almost anywhere in the world. They are, obviously, most expensive in Germany, where they represent the beginning of the great toy industry that developed from the folk art of Seiffen and the southern regions.

The clowns, roundabouts, and crying babies in cradles all became larger as the century progressed and complete dolls rather than the simple constructions of wood and wire were employed. Those made *c*1900 are particularly collectable, as they are very decorative. Dolls with pretty bisque heads swing garlands of flowers above their heads, dance under arches, play musical instruments or ride in a sleigh or on a roundabout. Sometimes the products of several manufacturers are combined in a single piece: the dolls' heads from Simon & Halbig or Armand Marseille, the skin-covered horses by F. Graeffer or Louis Lindner and the musical movements provided by one of the specialist firms based at Marburg in Hesse.

Most of these tinkle-box automata, often described as manivelle-operated, are covered with marbled or patterned paper that is sometimes further decorated with flowered or embossed gold borders. Pretty children and animals were the most popular subjects and kittens have tea at a small table, bears dance and dogs and elephants perform simple tricks. A simple construction could be made up in a variety of ways, by substituting bisque dolls' heads for cats or bears and changing the colour of the clothes and the patterned papers on the base. Few of the individual manufacturers of such toys are known and when a piece does carry a mark it usually relates to the seller rather than the maker. Because of the time needed to assemble, paint and finish such ephemeral items, they were produced only when peasant labour was very cheap and their quality declined sharply after 1910, when workers came to demand a better standard of living.

OPPOSITE *William Britain was one of the few British firms to produce automata. The Automatic Foot Race was marketed by the firm in the 1880s. The heads and limbs are made of lead and the figures are costumed in fabric. The central column is covered with lithographed paper. The two men race around, passing and repassing one another.*

LEFT *Simple squeak toys, sold extremely cheaply, were made in vast numbers in Sonneberg and Seiffen. Some have the sound mechanism in the neck, while others perform one movement, such as nodding or wagging the tail.*

French manivelle-operated toys are often so similar to those made in Germany that they can be differentiated only by their decorative detail or, sometimes, their subject-matter. As relatively few French dolls' heads were exported to Germany, any examples with marked French bisque heads are attributed to France. The problem is further complicated by the fact that many French assemblers often used German dolls, which were cheaper. The collector has, therefore, usually to be satisfied with the loose term 'French type'. Among the subjects that were made in France are farmyards, stables and twirling dancing children. One amusing scene showed a cook working in front of an oven. When the lid of a pan is lifted, out runs a mouse.

Father Christmas was an especially popular subject, large versions of which were an important feature in window displays in December. Automated white-bearded figures ride in sleighs or simple motor cars. They are valued by their appearance rather than their place of origin, though examples containing a musical movement are more expensive. Some of the display automata are deceptively old in appearance, as *papier-mâché* heads, have continued to be used for limited production items to the present day. Negro minstrels, clowns, Japanese ladies and tea-drinking Chinese have remained popular since the mid-19th century. Some subjects were specially made for butchers, fishmongers and shoe repairers. Gnome cobblers and old gentlemen, sometimes carrying the name of the shop or the product, often appear in the auction rooms and are popular with collectors of advertising material.

Because of the high price of good French automata, many collectors now concentrate on manivelle-type boxes or advertising figures, which are still relatively cheap.

PROBLEMS OF EVALUATION

TOP-QUALITY AUTOMATA have to be purchased with extreme caution or expert advice. They are a minefield for the novice. Among the many problems are replacement heads, simplified or changed mechanisms and marriages of sections from other structures. The musical movement, which can be concealed in a 'landscape' base or fitted into the body of the automaton, is sometimes found to be a modern replacement. Experienced collectors prefer to buy examples in completely original condition, even if the piece is not fully in working order. They are especially wary of pieces that have been thoroughly cleaned and re-costumed; enthusiastic restoration can cause irrevocable damage.

Valuing automata can be difficult. Some models that look very impressive are in fact fairly common, while others with less immediate appeal have rarity value. Any old automaton in original condition, even if it is one of the more common types, is well worth buying, since relatively few models come up for sale internationally each year. Some guidance as to current market values is provided in the estimates which are published in auction room catalogues, though the buyer should remember that the cataloguer might not be an expert in this field and is unlikely to have risked damage to the costume by opening the figure to examine the mechanism. In general, new collectors are advised to buy from an automata specialist, who will provide a written guarantee with the piece and will be willing to supervise any restoration that might be needed in the future. Unfortunately doll dealers also sell automata which they value more on the quality and make of the head and costume rather than the mechanism, in which they are often uninterested. Occasionally the figure is worth more as a doll than as an automaton — yet another problem for the new collector.

Simpler clockwork toys are not a problem as anyone with a basic knowledge of them can satisfy themselves that the piece has not been tampered with. The degree of restoration and re-costuming that is acceptable to collectors varies between countries and locality. In France, complete originality of costume is most important, whereas in the United States a completely re-dressed item will sell well. Attitudes in Great Britain and Germany vary and there are collectors in both countries who re-costume any figures that are not in pristine condition. However, as interest in conservation increases, fewer automata will be unnecessarily restored, but this will also demand a higher degree of expertise on the part of the owner.

Though damage puts off the leading dealers in automata, very distressed items often fetch high prices when they are purchased speculatively by non-specialists, many of whom are unaware of the very high cost of good restoration. There are specialist restorers of automata in all countries, but it is advisable to use someone who has been recommended by a satisfied client. Anyone can set up as a restorer and some dis-

astrous work is sometimes carried out on valuable pieces. Some restorers, more interested in the mechanical side of the figure than the costume, repair the movements at the expense of the textiles; others pretty up the clothes to such an extent that the figure looks modern. In general, it is best to ask for advice from a collectors' club, a museum or a reputable dealer. Before leaving the piece with a restorer, insist that the costume remain intact and that any replacement, as opposed to mending, of parts be undertaken only after consultation. The best restorers list the work they have undertaken on their bill, which should be retained with the figure to assist when future work has to be done.

The automata market remains very stable. Once hooked, enthusiasts rarely abandon the speciality. They also keep pieces for a long time, so that few come on the market. Each year, the number of good automata sold internationally declines, forcing up prices and making these aristocrats of the toy world very attractive as long-term investments.

ABOVE *A group of mid-19th-century, German wheeled-toys of fine quality, with one or two movements such as for plucking a harp or twirling a hoop. These papier-mâché headed toys were costumed in fabrics and were activated by wires attached to the wheeled bases. This page is from a German toy merchant's catalogue, showing hand-coloured illustrations.*

METAL TOYS

IGURES AND TABLEAUX that were made from a mixture of materials, such as *papier mâché*, wood and metal, were very labour-intensive and made commercial sense only if they were produced for the luxury market. As the work force, especially in Germany, became more organized and demanded better pay and working conditions, traditional toys, largely made by domestic outworkers, were gradually replaced by factory products. By the mid-19th century, children were also becoming more selective and the old folk-style coach and horses carved from wood no longer satisfied a child who was interested in the fine detail of contemporary transport, detail that could be reproduced only in a material strong enough to cut in fine outline, embossed and twisted to create a realistic sleigh, brougham or boat.

Many of the small toymaking firms, especially in France, worked in mean backrooms, converting scrap metal into quaint, cleverly made pieces. Toys of this type, including a large number of kitchen pieces, are rarely marked, but they were made in quantity in Britain and the United States, as well as the more established centres of Paris and Nuremberg-Fürth. Many tin toys continued to be made in small single-

family workshops until World War I. Such work was never marked; it has to be valued purely on appearance and quality of workmanship.

The majority of metal toymaking firms had factories that were divided into sheet-metal rooms, tool rooms, moulding and pressing areas and painting rooms. The most skilled, and the most highly paid, craftsmen were those who lined the detail on coaches and motor vehicles. By 1900 the large German firms had steam and electrical workshops, packing rooms and stores, as well as studios where the toys and their packages were designed.

The commercial production of metal toys began in Germany in the 18th century, but the great advance came after 1850, thanks to continual improvements in machinery and communications. Mass-production was not possible until factories were powered by steam and, later, electricity; nor was it possible to deliver up-to-date models to the retailers until the railway system was well established. The more complex toys, because of the expensive tooling of their parts, were not suitable for family workshops. They were the province of the large factories who were proud to mark their work. The Germans were particularly skilled in merchandizing and

OPPOSITE TOP *Airships captured the imagination of the public during the early years of the 20th century. The Lehmann factory produced the model illustrated here, the EPL II, in two sizes. The celluloid propellor pushed the airship, when suspended from a string, in circles.*

OPPOSITE BOTTOM *A fine live-steam model of a liner, made by Gebrüder Bing of Nuremberg c1912. It flies French flags and is in good condition, showing only minor flaking.*

LEFT *Gebrüder Bing was one of the first German makers to produce a variety of motor cars. This hand-painted Brake, reminiscent of horse-drawn traps in its seating arrangement, was made c1904.*

were quick to see the importance of adapting exported toys: Nuremberg-made buses and delivery vehicles carry British or American advertisements and ships bear names that were familiar in London nurseries.

Despite improvements in decorating techniques, which made metal toys more colourful, the majority, especially in the United States, were still hand-painted in 1900, though the surface was sometimes further decorated with stencils, transfers or sprayed effects. This continued use of what were really outdated techniques gives many tin toys a deceptive antique appearance. All the manufacturers cloaked their methods of printing on tin in great secrecy and it is still impossible to know exactly how some effects were achieved. Printing in colours by a lithographic process had been in use since the mid-19th century, but it was not in general use on tinplate toys until 1900. The old lithographic process, involving the use of colour on a stone, was not suitable for printing on metal, but rapid improvements in specialized techniques after 1875, especially in the field of roller printing, made the

process viable. It became much cheaper after 1900, when metal lithoplates were used instead of stones, and even more economical in the 1920s, when photo-lithography began to be used.

HORSE-DRAWN TRANSPORT

THE EARLIEST HIGHLY collectable tin toys represent the various types of horse-drawn transport. Some of these pieces are surprisingly large and have perfectly constructed detail in leather, brass, and fabric, which brings them close in spirit to automata. Caleches, mail coaches, broughams and hackney carriages were made in Germany and France, some of the finest measuring 24in (60cm) in length. These were expensive toys and the detail was finely executed, as the aim was to create a realistic model. The horses are sometimes made of wood or skin over wood, *papier mâché*, composition or even zinc; the trappings and harness are often beautifully made miniatures. Some of the paintwork is also highly detailed, with enamelled and lacquered panels, those on coaches sometimes embellished with a coat of arms or a monogram. The superb quality of these horse-drawn toys can also be seen in the makers' attention to specific effects, such as embossed springs or satin-upholstered interiors.

Occasionally carriages are found with their original drivers and passengers, whose costumes provide one of the best methods of dating the toys. Some of the most elegant date from the Regency period and are, obviously, fairly rare. Curiously, despite their high quality and early date, toys of this type sell for less than the motor cars made by firms such as Märklin after 1900.

OPPOSITE TOP *Many of the early models of cars were not based on recognizable prototypes. This tinplate tourer, made by Gebrüder Bing c1902, is hand-painted in great detail and still has its original amber glass headlamps.*

OPPOSITE BOTTOM *Chad Valley of England produced toys in a variety of materials including tinplate. This model of a delivery van, dating to the 1930s, carried various advertising slogans for the games produced by the firm.*

Carriages, as well as tin furniture for dolls' houses, were produced by one of the oldest-established German toy-makers, Ludwig Lutz of Ellwangen. This firm, founded in 1846, specialized in toys of high quality, but somewhat fragile construction; they appear never to have been marked. Some of the finest early horse-drawn toys are often attributed to Rock & Graner, founded in Biberach an der Riss in 1913. This Württemberg firm produced toys at a small factory and used a variety of metals, including copper and sheet zinc. At the Great Exhibition in London in 1851 the firm was awarded a Prize Medal. At this time the factory was producing *papier mâché* as well as tin toys and its fame rested mainly on its tinplate fountains and other water toys. The company made

BELOW *Although unmarked, this toy is obviously of high quality. The body pressings are detailed, suggesting deep buttoning on the upholstery. Hand-enamelled, it is in excellent condition.*

ABOVE *A good example of a pre World War I closed landaulet, with the chauffeur sitting in the open. The steering wheel is turned to make the car run in a circle.*

RIGHT *Lithography and hand-painting were used to decorate this toy — a rare combination of techniques during this period. It is an extremely early car, made c1898, and was produced by the Hess firm. It has brass plaques bearing the German patent number.*

LEFT *Steam, as a means of powering full-sized cars, had almost completely died out before World War I, making this live-steam model, made by the German firm of Doll et Cie c1924, especially interesting.*

BELOW *Made by Bing in the early 1920s, this limousine, featuring a chauffeur, was fitted with electric headlights for added realism. By this period all decorative detail was lithographed.*

steam carriages as well as clockwork, steam ships and dolls'-house furniture. Railways later became its main product.

Exceptionally good German carriages are now frequently attributed to Rock and Graner, but they could equally well have been made by any of the small factories producing quality toys. The most lavishly finished carriages were made in France in the last quarter of the 19th century, with folding leather hoods, silver-plated lamps and satin upholstery. They are rarely marked, but sometimes carry the label of the shop where they were sold. Any tinplate toys of this type, especially those in the larger sizes, are now rare and expensive. They were time-consuming to produce and were never made in large numbers. But the ability to make a detailed carriage proved the skill of a young apprentice, and these pieces, treasured in German families, occasionally appear in exhibitions.

As horse-drawn transport was common in town and country until the late 1930s, toymakers continued to produce fire-engines, milk-floats, mail-coaches, trams and street-cleaning carts. Some are curiously archaic in style, such as those made by the French firm of Charles Rossignol between 1920 and 1930. Despite the number of motor vehicles on the

roads, Rossignol, in company with many German and American firms, continued to make painted tinplate cabs, water carts and farm and military pieces. Some of the horse-drawn transport was sold complete with a tinplate or wooden stable, fire station or store, though few have survived complete.

Donkeys, reindeer, goats and dogs are all found pulling decorative road vehicles, as well as fairground and circus items. It is sometimes possible to attribute unmarked pieces by reference to catalogues, but in general these toys are valued mainly by their age and visual appeal. Those made after 1920 tend to be very simple: the horses are often two sections tabbed together and lithographed. Even so, many of them have a primitive charm and they are now becoming collectable. More recently, Japanese-made horses have appeared, indicating the continual appeal of this old-fashioned form of transport.

TOY MOTOR CARS

WHEN MOTOR CARS first appeared on the roads, toy manufacturers were slow to accept their potential. Models were rarely seen in the shops before 1905. Motor vehicles are now, however, the most heavily collected area of tinplate, and pre-World War I pieces by known makers arouse international interest. By 1910 the makers were fully aware of the sales value of an up-to-the-minute toy and coupés, tourers, racing cars and double phaetons were put into production, the best of them having well-finished interiors, specially made miniature lamps and, occasionally, luggage and travelling rugs. The finest models, such as those made by the German firm, Märklin, are of heavy construction and often contain passengers. Because of the painted finish, it was possible to imitate the coach-lining of actual cars, making the models especially elegant. Originality of paintwork is very important in this area of metal-toy collecting, as the soft patina of age is impossible to reproduce.

RIGHT MAIN PICTURE *Gebrüder Märklin used a wealth of detail in the pressing and hand-painting of this touring motor. Four separate paint colours were used as well as gold coach lining, making it a most striking toy.*

RIGHT (INSET) *This Carette model of a Mercedes tourer was made c1907. It is unusual to find an example complete with its sidelights, reminiscent of carriage lamps. It also has headlights.*

BELOW *Although unmarked, this good example of a landaulet was probably made by Georges Carette c1911. The detail was lithographed and the model retains its full complement of nickel-plated lights.*

The first toy cars, such as those made in France in the 1890s by H. Vichy, with velvet and silk seats, are accurate copies of the horseless carriages. They are so rare that possession remains a dream for most collectors. Other makers produced motors with either civilian or military occupants in the years before World War I, but, judging from the small numbers illustrated in contemporary catalogues, they remained a relatively insignificant line among the traditional horse-drawn items.

After the war, due to simplified methods of production, cars became much cheaper to produce, and as they became available to a wider social group, children wanted copies of the newest models they saw in the street. Manufacturers were pleased to satisfy this demand with an ever-increasing assortment of toy cars in all sizes and prices. The majority of collectors now concentrate on the period between the wars, examples from which are available at all antique toy shows

OPPOSITE TOP *By the late 1920s, when this model of an open tourer was made in Germany by Johann Distler, the construction of model cars was much more flimsy and all paintwork was lithographed.*

OPPOSITE BOTTOM *The German firm of Märklin specialized in producing toys of superb quality, adding such features as a brass trim to the bonnet and a pierced metal radiator grill as shown in this model. Made c1907, this car must have been the finest model available in the toyshops.*

BELOW *Although unmarked, this good example of a landaulet was probably made by Georges Carette c1911. The detail was lithographed and the model retains its full complement of nickel-plated lights.*

and fairs. Though the detail and individual craftsmanship
that characterized the early models disappeared, the later
versions provide a fascinating miniature document of the
evolution of the car. Fortunately, the majority carry a maker's
mark.

All collectors have a preference for some particular
maker's work. Some like Bing and Märklin for their strength
and solidity, others prefer the whimsy of Lehmann or the
more romantic approach of Gunthermann, whose drivers
and passengers display charming detail such as minute
glasses or gloves. The work of Georges Carette is universally
popular, as his toys were both well made and designed with
true elegance and flair.

Carette, who was French by birth, the son of a Parisian
photographer, founded his toymaking firm, George Carette
& Cie, in Nuremberg in 1886 when he was only 24 years old.
He had learned the trade by serving an apprenticeship in the
large Bing factory and he remained especially interested in
the marketing and business side of his factory. He was always
keen to produce a striking toy at a competitive price and his
motor cars, though not as extravagant as those of Gunthermann, are beautifully decorated in attractive colours. His firm
expanded rapidly and by 1900 had depots all over Europe and
employed some 400 people.

In 1911 Carette headed his range of cards with a superb Motor Landaulette with reversing gears and a brake. This motor, complete with a painted *papier-mâché* chauffeur, could be adjusted for straight or circular running and was beautifully finished with nickelled head lamps and rubber-tyred wheels. The company sold boxes of assorted figures, so that a convincingly crowded effect could be achieved. These figures were especially useful for the motor buses, for which special conductors and drivers were made. One of the buses carried English advertisements and was marketed as a London bus. It remains one of the most popular Carette toys.

Delivery vans, water lorries and mail vans were produced by Carette as well as tinplate garages that could have a workbench and vice fitted. Almost all worked either by a clockwork spring motor or a flywheel. Carette's fire station, sold with three vehicles, had a working water jet and hose as well as removable figures.

During World War I Carette was forced to return to his native France, although the company continued to trade until 1917, when its stock and tools were dispersed, some of the cars later appearing with the Karl Bub trademark. Bub was another Nuremberg firm, founded in 1851, and reaching its peak of production in the 1920s, when large numbers of saloon cars and tourers of fairly light construction were made. In 1935, to celebrate the centenary of the Nuremberg-Fürth railway, an amusingly atavistic train with printed period occupants was made.

The most revered German maker is Märklin, a firm that is still in operation and still producing fine-quality toys. Many of its early toys are more light-hearted than those of Carette and have painted detail that seems to have been added purely for love of decoration. The company was established in Württemburg in 1859 and originally concentrated on metal toys for dolls' rooms and kitchens. The early years, when the business was largely run by Carolyn, the wife of the founder, Theodor Märklin, were difficult. In 1888 a new company, Gebrüder Märklin (1900-63) recorded that business improved after the company took over the fine-quality products of Ludwig Lutz. New capital was injected in 1892 and the firm changed its name to Gebrüder Märklin & Co., a name that was retained until 1907. The company expanded rapidly, new premises were taken on and another old toy-making firm, Rock & Graner, absorbed. Because of financial problems another partner was taken on in 1907 and the name again changed to Gebrüder Märklin & Cie.

After the Lutz take-over, the range of Märklin toys increased dramatically and there was tremendous concentration on transport vehicles. They were made in heavy tinplate and in the somewhat severe classic German style. Unlike Carette, Märklin did not produce a great variety of cars, so that any examples coming on the market are very desirable. By painting vehicles in different colours and adding special detail, the same model could assume a new identity: a passenger car, for instance, can become a taxi. Most Märklin toys of the great era, between 1895 and 1914, were hand-made in heavy metal and some have extravagant detail, such as leather luggage straps and removable spare tyres. This attention to detail is seen on the boats. Some decks have slots into which semi-flat model sailors can be fixed, so that they remain in position even when the models are floated.

LEFT *Although the instruction leaflet shows steam coming from the funnel of this fishing boat, it was actually fly-wheel powered, as can be seen from the handle at the stern. Made by Ueberlacker of Nuremberg in the late 1880s.*

BELOW *A highly detailed clockwork-powered riverboat, the Greiff, made by Georges Carette in Germany c1902. Considerable detail has been packed into the small vessel, which still has its well-made lifeboats.*

TOY BOATS

EVERY TOY COLLECTOR dreams of owning one of the boats made by a firm such as Märklin before World War I. Some of these fine toys measure more than 40in (100cm) and were powered by clockwork, electricity or steam. As the boats were intended to be floated, few have survived in good condition. Some of the clockwork versions could run for over a quarter of an hour, while the steam-powered *Mauretania* could travel for an hour. No wonder so many were lost as they ploughed their way into the centre of lakes and ponds! Even if the boat returned to the nursery, it was often put away wet and allowed to rust. Inevitably, such toys are extremely rare and the survival of examples complete with their sailors, lifeboats and fabric flags is almost miraculous.

By 1891 Märklin was producing a range of boats alongside its elegant horse-drawn carriages and military vehicles. Some of these early models continued in production for many years, such as the steam yachts and paddle steamers; but it is the large battleships and torpedo boats, powered by steam or clockwork, that have become the stars for collectors. The passenger steamers and naval craft offered by the firm after the war were not so lavishly equipped as the early products, and detail, such as sailors that could be fixed in position, disappeared. The ocean liner, *Columbus*, some 40in (100cm) long, with a powerful motor, could run for 12 minutes and was fitted with forward and reverse movement. All the boats had adjustable steering gear and were sold with stands for display in the nursery. Some of the larger sizes were very expensive

and were owned by the richest children; production was limited. Despite the war-weariness of the European public, torpedo boats, battleships and gunboats remained popular toys. Submarines, which dived automatically at intervals, ranged in size from 9½ to 30in (23 to 75cm); it is the small sizes that are now commonly found.

Carette boats are much rarer than those produced by Märklin. They were very well made, with a japanned finish, and the larger sizes, such as ocean-going steamships, were supplied with an anchor and chain as well as lifeboats. In order to make German-designed vessels acceptable in Great Britain and the United States, they were given non-German names. Large pleasure steamers, coasting cruisers with quick-firing guns, searchlight and look-out stations and torpedo boats

with signalling apparatus were available by 1911. In lighter vein there were pleasure yachts and a splendid despatch boat, the *Sleipner*, that was advertised as a scale model of the ship in attendance on the German emperor.

The other great German toymaker, Gebrüder Bing, also made high-quality boats and submarines, though they do not rival the finest Märklin pieces. The early Bing boats, dating from 1895 to 1910, are the best, with painted detail and lavish ornament added for the enjoyment of the buyer. As Bing, unlike Carette, marked its work, the firm is especially popular with collectors. Some Bing toys, such as the smaller submarines, are not very expensive, as they have survived in some quantity; but larger boats, if in good condition, can comman extremely high prices.

The brothers Ignaz and Adolf Bing began producing tinplate kitchenware and toys in the 1960s in Nuremberg, but little is known about the firm's early products, because real expansion began only in the 1890s, when the firm became a limited company. The Bing brothers were excellent businessmen and their products were on sale across the world, from Sudan to Alaska. They also saw the importance of displaying their latest toys at international exhibitions, and any medals won at such exhibitions could be used in advertising. Their finest boats were sold in specially designed presentation boxes, with a seascape forming a realistic background. Others

OPPOSITE TOP *Dating to the 1920s, the Jolanda is an attractive model of a large yacht. Made in Germany by Gebrüder Märklin, the advent of radio was recognized by the aerial strung between the masts.*

OPPOSITE BOTTOM *This model of a German submarine, made by Gebrüder Bing of Nuremberg, is in fine condition, still retaining its national and Kriegsmarine flags. The clockwork motor, which makes the vessel dive and surface repeatedly, is wound through the screw fitting in the conning tower.*

were sold in strong wooden boxes (sometimes marked with the name of the retailer, such as Gamages) and they owe their survival after years of neglect in attics and basements to this rigid packaging.

Both Bing and Märklin made some boats that were three ft (one m) long and by 1912 Bing was producing automatically-firing gunboats, torpedo boats and destroyers powered by steam or the more expensive clockwork. All Bing toys made before 1919 carry the mark 'GBN'; after that date 'B.W.' *(Bing Werke)* is found. The firm went into receivership in 1932. Bing Werke toys lack the allure of the early work, as they are more economically made to compete with the products of other toymakers in the difficult years of the Depression. But since the early pieces are now very expensive, the cars, steam accessories and boats made in the later period are becoming more popular.

LEHMANN TINPLATE TOYS

LEHMANN, A FIRM that was established in Brandenburg in 1881, approached the problem of creating models of contemporary transport in a light-hearted way and concentrated, not on accuracy and good quality, but on surface decoration and novelty. As the toys made by this company were so much cheaper than those made by Bing or Carette, they were

ABOVE *Clockwork-powered, this model of a torpedo boat was made by Gebrüder Bing of Nuremberg c 1910. Lacking its mast and funnel, it represented a very fast class of boat that was thought to be a major threat to capital ships.*

owned by children of all income levels. Many models have survived in number, depressing their price. For Lehmann designers a simple car was not enough: it had to be occupied by a naughty boy who drove it erratically. As Lehmann toys are marked both with the name of the firm and with design patent details, they are immediately recognizable. Sometimes the company name was added to a toy even though it detracted from the overall effect — as on an airship or a bus, where the patent mark is carried on the bonnet.

Buses, trucks, animals and vans, all decorated in bright, eye-catching colours, poured out of the Lehmann factory after 1900. Many of these charming creations resemble automata in being so cleverly designed, presumably so that adults would find them irresistible and carry them home as gifts for children. A stubborn mule, with a comical clown attempting to control a bucking donkey that pulls a circus cart, is the most famous of the firm's products.

By the 1920s Lehmann was producing more than 80 different models, most of them carrying a name such as 'Halloh', a boy riding a motor bike, 'Mandarin', with two bearers car-

OPPOSITE TOP *H.M.S. Barfleur was made in Germany by Gebrüder Märklin c1924. Steam-powered, the ship has three propellers and a formidable array of guns.*

OPPOSITE BOTTOM *Much cheaper and more crudely made is this small representation of a passenger liner of the 1920s. Unmarked, it is clockwork powered and wound by the large key at the stern.*

BELOW *An impressive hand-painted model liner, the Kaiserin Augusta Victoria, made c1912 by Gebrüder Märklin, is in its original state. The ship carries eight lifeboats.*

rying a sedan chair, 'Tut-tut', a car, and the much rarer 'Baker and Sweep', with a sweep attacking the baker. Many of these toys remained on the market for long periods and their patents were re-applied for. As this information is printed on the tinplate, most Lehmann toys are fairly easy to date. In 1921 the firm had some 800 workers and was at its peak of production; by then Johann Richter had become a partner, a man who had studied working methods in other countries and was full of new ideas. After World War II, the Lehmann factory was sequestered by the Soviet Union, but Richter re-established the toymaking firm near Nuremberg and it is still in production.

Because of their somewhat flimsy construction, Lehmann toys are sometimes ignored by top collectors, who prefer the weight and solemnity of Carette or Märklin transport vehicles. Yet arranged as a group, especially if with their colourful original boxes, Lehmann toys are visually arresting, full of humour and incident. Some of the designs introduced before 1900 are extremely progressive, so simple that they might have been made in the 1920s. *Gustav the Miller*, who climbs a pole and sets the sails of his mill in action, was first sold in 1897, yet must have looked completely up-to-date to boys in the 1930s. Some of the firm's products were such good sellers they were produced for a long period of time. They are relatively common and fetch low prices. Others, such as the amphibious car, patented in 1905, are much rarer and make excellent investments.

Despite their apparent fragility of construction, some Lehmann toys performed extremely well, with motors that could run for an hour. The mechanical airship show, composed of dirigibles and aeroplanes circling a tower, was a continuous spectacle, as was their *County Fair Tower*, with cars running under arches while airships circle above, a toy that was introduced in 1914.

AIRSHIPS AND AEROPLANES

BEFORE 1914 THERE were relatively few aeroplanes made as toys, perhaps because the manufacturers felt that they were too remote from the daily lives of most boys. Pre-1914 models are rare and desirable, even if their condition is not superb. As Carette ceased trading in 1917, before any toymaker created planes in great numbers, their work is especially valuable.

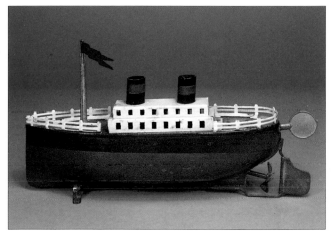

During its short years of production, the Carette firm concentrated as much on airships such as Zeppelins as on planes. Their Parseval airship, in the larger sizes, had two propellers that helped the craft describe wide circles. Carette's 1911 catalogue showed only two aeroplanes: Wright-type biplanes and the Blériot monoplane, a curiously fragile construction.

The exploits of daring pilots during World War I attracted the imagination of boys all over the world and toy manufacturers encouraged their interest with an assortment of aeroplanes modelled, not only on the latest designs of the 1920s, but on the fighter planes of the war years. Aeroplanes, like ships, had a hard time in the nursery and they are rarely found in good condition. They are, even so, popular with collectors; they look effective when suspended over model cars and trains and are good decorative pieces for display in a study or a bedroom.

After the famous solo crossing of the Atlantic by Charles Lindbergh in 1927, interest in model planes increased and by 1930 there were planes that had parachutes, planes with tinplate hangers and planes which circled over ships or aerodromes. The German firms Gunthermann, Lehmann, Distler, and Tipp all made quite accurate models of civil and military aircraft, as well as seaplanes. Some of these toys were made of very thin tinplate; it looked effective when it was freshly lithographed, but it soon dented and rusted. The penny-toy versions, so small that they were usually played with indoors, have often lasted better.

PENNY TOYS FOR THE MASS MARKET

'PENNY TOYS' IS the popular term for a variety of brightly coloured figures, animals and transport vehicles that were made in France and Germany until the 1930s. The most collectable are those made before World War I; their colouring is much richer and they have more embossed detail. Some have moving parts — a football that is kicked between two players, hens that peck at their food or a clown who beats a donkey.

Many of them were produced over a long period and have to be dated by their colour and the general quality of their construction. Relatively few are marked, as they were made by dozens of small firms who sold their products through the big Nuremberg wholesalers, such as Moses Kohnstam, who traded as Moko.

In the 1928-30 Moko catalogue are found horse-drawn carriages and Edwardian rowing boats, alongside up-to-the-minute cars, sewing machines and motor bikes. Some of the penny toys, such as the trains, were made in several pieces and were originally sold boxed. Those made by the French firm, Rossignol, were marketed in this way, though the majority of makers seem to have sold the pieces loose and by the gross to street hawkers and sweet-shops.

A light-hearted, amusing approach was necessary for any firm producing penny toys. French toymakers, in particular, seemed to have the ability to make a model, perhaps from scrap materials, eye-catching and magical. While the raw materials used for the French penny toys might be of the cheapest kind, the decoration and finish is always delicate and charming. As they were made in small workshops in the back streets of Paris, the toys are rarely marked.

METAL TOY PRODUCTION IN FRANCE

MANY OF THE toys made by the larger factories retain a lightness of touch that provides a contrast with the more serious work of Bing or Carette. This typically French approach is seen particularly in the products of Fernand Martin, who founded his Paris factory in 1878. Like Lehmann, the most whimsical of the German makers, Martin created amusing figures that reflect scenes in the streets, in shops or the circus; but instead of covering the surface with bright lithography, he aimed at greater realism and even costumed some figures in fabric.

Martin was also especially interested in the advertising and sales potential of attractive boxes and these carry the name of the toy and the maker, as well as the dates of the medals he was awarded at international exhibitions.

Though the construction of Martin toys — a combination of wire, steel, copper, lead and fabric — seems complex and time-consuming, the firm was profitable, partly because the same models were made year after year with different finishes or detail to suit foreign markets. One toy, *The Sheriff*, seems to have been specially made in 1892 for the Chicago World Fair, presumably because of the success Martin had achieved with previous toys such as a jazz band and a wheelchair that were made for French exhibitions. Drunkards, street violinists, waiters, boxers, policemen, fruit-sellers, concierges and laundrywomen, all caricaturing Parisian daily life, poured out of the Martin factory. Some of these toys now appeal more to automata enthusiasts than tin-toy collectors, but they also offer a large collecting field in their own right.

Martin was fascinated by the history of toys and he gave the Conservatoire des Arts et Métiers in Paris a large collection of the toys he had made over a 30-year period — the only 19th-century toymaker to have foreseen the historical importance of his work.

Some of the best-quality French tin toys were made by Jouets de Paris, a firm that in the 1920s and 1930s produced models of all the famous cars of the period. Their *Hispano Suiza* was an impressive 20½in (52cm) long and was fitted

RIGHT *Made in the immediate post-war period, this novelty toy of a porter driving a luggage trolley is brightly lithographed and marked 'Made in the US Zone of Germany'. He pursues an erratic course when wound.*

BELOW *Clockwork-powered, this German railway porter was made c1910 by Walter Stock of Solingen, a German firm specializing in the manufacture of novelty toys.*

LEFT *Although unmarked, this tinplate money box is obviously German and dates to the 1950s. When the lever at the side is pulled, the woodsman hits the coin with his axe so that it falls into the base.*

OPPOSITE *The fine detail of this tinplate phaeton makes it extremely attractive. Unmarked, it was made in Germany c1870, probably by Lutz.*

RIGHT *Many toys made during the 1930s were only marked on their boxes. This vehicle, powered by clockwork, is a well-made example of this period.*

BELOW *Tinplate toys, such as kitchens and bathrooms, were specifically made for girls. This example, made in Germany, has a working tap supplied from a tank on the back wall.*

with lights; and the Delage racing car was claimed to be 'the prettiest racing car ever'. Most of the firm's products are clearly marked and they are well worth collecting. The quality, even of toys from the late period, is always good. The company is believed to have originated in Paris in 1899 as the Société Industrielle de Ferblanterie, the name being changed to Jouets de Paris in 1928 and to Jouets en Paris (J.E.P.) in 1932. The finest toys were undoubtedly made in the 1930s. The Rolls Royce is a superb model that is both strongly and accurately made.

Their greatest French competitor in the area of model cars was Citroën, who, in the early 1920s, decided to use copies of their automobiles as promotional items. Both pick-up trucks and cars were made by Citroën, with the aim of encouraging children to know the maker's name from their earliest years. Attractive posters showing infants with the toy cars helped boost sales — some 15,000 in 1923, the first year of production. In 1928, 'miniature toys' that were die-cast appeared on the market and were an immediate success. The tinplate delivery vans, taxis, coupés and flat-bed lorries were quite accurate copies and could be purchased from car show-rooms or shops. They were frequently issued at the same time as a new full-sized automobile, so that children could encourage papa to acquire the latest model.

The B2 taxi, with canework panels to the passenger section, is one of the most collectable pieces, though the B2 Torpedo, being the first to be made in 1923, is also popular. Virtually all the models carry the Citroën trademark and are easily identifiable. The good products were made for a relatively short period, as fewer were marketed in the late 1930s (though a small range was made after the war by another company).

Another great French maker of tinplate toys was Charles Rossignol, who began production in *c.* 1888 in Paris. Like Citroën products, the firm's models were always marked and the boxes also carried the company's monogram. Production ceased as recently as 1962, leaving collectors a very wide

range of models and styles from which to choose. The earliest products are believed to have been floor trains, but motor cars, horse-drawn vehicles, field ambulances, steam boats and well-made penny toys were also produced. Friction-driven milk carts, with drivers and a group of churns, are among the most decorative pieces, though their clockwork taxi-cabs, limousines and coupés, with bright lithography, are more generally popular with collectors and attract the highest prices. Some Rossignol toys, such as their steam fire-pumps were lacquered, not lithographed, but all are clearly marked with a monogram. In several instances, indeed, the monogram is an integral part of the surface decoration.

THE BRITISH AND AMERICAN MANUFACTURERS

SOME CLOCKWORK TOYS were also made in Great Britain as early as the 18th century, but the industry never attained the strength that might have been expected, mainly because of the high cost of labour. As a result of the cessation of imports from Germany during World War I, the tin toy industry was forced into life. Previously, tin and metal toys had been produced in Birmingham and Wolverhampton, but these were

OPPOSITE *An unmarked figure representing Charlie Chaplin, made c1930. Dressed in felt clothes, he characteristically shuffles along, twirling his cane.*

LEFT *Known as* La Conquête du Nord, *this toy was inspired by the expedition of the American Admiral Peary. Made c1909 by Fernand Martin in France.*

BELOW *Although called Snoopy, this bloodhound seems earlier than the American comic-strip character. Marked 'Made in Britain', he wags his tail as he pursues his quarry.*

mainly for dolls' houses, model kitchens and the seaside. William Britain, in the 1880s, had produced some inventive metal toys such as an equestrienne, and they are highly collectable, but the best period for the collector is after 1930, when firms such as Wells, Hornby, Chad Valley and Mettoy were in full production. Few of the British makers before 1914 marked their work, as it was sold very cheaply directly to the retailers. James Norris of Birmingham was one of the leading makers of toy scales and dolls' kitchenware, while The Fancy Toy Company in the same city specialized in tin gardening tools and sand moulds for turrets and battlements.

The finest tinplate kitchenware had been made in Germany by firms such as Märklin, who created a series of spirit and gas-fired kitchen ranges that were beautifully finished as functional items. British output was unexciting by comparison and it was not until the 1930s that well-finished, cleverly designed pieces appeared in quantity. The quality of British printing on tinplate was good, as is evidenced by the very attractive biscuit tins and containers that were made before 1910, but these skills were not at first directed towards toy transport. Some of the best model cars were made by Brimtoy, who used Nelson's column as the company trademark. This firm later amalgamated with Wells to become Wells Brimtoy, the main British producer of lithographed toys until the late 1950s.

Though many of the road vehicles made in the 1920s and 1930s seem light and poorly made in comparison with the classic French and German products of the turn of the century, they now have a following of their own. Mettoy, Tri-ang, Sutcliffe, Crescent Toys and Chad Valley all made models of contemporary road vehicles that were finished in bright colours. The Tri-ang toys are of a much plainer construction, without the lithography that made the Chad Valley pieces so lively, and were usually stove-enamelled.

OPPOSITE *Dating to the 1930s and obviously of British manufacture, this representation of the guards outside Buckingham Palace is well lithographed and sturdily made. The soldiers 'march' up and down between the gates and their sentry boxes.*

RIGHT *Disney characters were obvious hits with film-going children. Goofy the Gardener made in Britain by Marx in the 1950s is brightly lithographed and 'walks' along, pushing his wheelbarrow.*

BELOW *Completely unmarked, this model of an English Green Line bus represented the ultimate in luxury coach travel of the period. Made in the 1930s, it is powered by a simple clockwork mechanism.*

Early American metal toymakers, like the British, concentrated on kitchenware and very simple toys; most of the rest were still imported from Europe. The native industry developed rapidly after 1840, with the main emphasis on cast-iron. The Americans were comparatively late in making use of lithography and many of the pieces made around the turn of the century were painted and stencilled in a deceptively atavistic manner. The toy industry boomed after 1900, though there were still fewer than 100 manufacturers. After World War I American production again increased and toy design became much more inventive. Manufacturers such as Louis Marx were eager to represent popular characters of the period such as Charlie MacCarthy, the ventriloquist's dummy, Donald Duck and Mickey Mouse, and every advance in transport and aeronautics was reflected in an accurate model.

The production of cast-iron toys, a peculiarly American activity, reached its peak in the 1880s. Money boxes, bell toys, horse-drawn transport, sleighs, animals and caricatures of politicians were all created in cast iron which could be poured into very complex moulds. In some early toys, tin and cast iron were used together and some of the finest bell toys, such as elephants who pivot to strike bells, were made of cast-iron. The first 100 years of American independence celebrated in 1876 fostered a spate of centennial toys, incorporating the Centennial Bell.

Because of the current interest in primitive art, American toys have become increasingly popular internationally and prices for some of the early pieces, such as those that appear in the George Brown Sketchbook of 1870, are now classed among the greats. George W. Brown & Co. was founded in

OPPOSITE *The best makers of tin toys in the period following World War II were the Japanese. This black Cadillac and Buick are of large size and accurately portray the garish appearance of American cars of the late 1950s.*

BELOW *Very simple in design and relying entirely on lithography for its appeal, this model of an Express Transport delivery van was made by Wells of London c1935.*

1856 in Connecticut. It was amalgamated with J. & E. Stephens in 1869 to form the Stephens & Brown Manufacturing Company. Brown made a number of boats, some of which appeared in a wheeled version as carpet toys. Delivery vehicles, circus cages, horses in hoops, birds that balance between large wheels, pull-along trains and very elegant wire-work hose-reel fire carriages were made by this prolific and versatile maker. Brown's toys are identified either by a label that was fixed to the boxes or by reference to the Sketchbook.

The cleverly designed, but decidedly lightweight, lithographed tinplate toys made by Louis Marx in the 20th century are a complete contrast to the heavy, primitive creations of George Brown, but they are equally typical of their period. Marx, born in 1894, originally worked for Ferdinand Strauss, one of the major American clockwork toymakers. After a rapid rise from office-boy to millionaire before the age of 30, Marx took over several factories and acquired the rights to some of the Strauss lines. He aimed to create toys for the new mass market which demanded novelty at low prices. One of the most memorable of his creations is the *Merrymakers Orchestra*, with four mice around a piano. By buying out most of his competitors in the 1930s, Marx became the largest toy-making firm in the world, concentrating on novelty items.

A similar approach to the mass market is apparent in the light, brightly coloured tin toys made in Japan. At first, Japanese products were mainly imitative, but after 1945 Japanese designers began to create more imaginative work. Well-tried clockwork mechanisms were cast aside in favour of battery-operated electric motors which were much more in tune with space-age rockets and moon landing craft. Some of the Japanese aeroplanes are superb, complex models of contemporary advances. In addition, a wide range of cheap novelty pieces flooded the shelves of chain stores, offering children a choice of anything from a ladybird to a helicopter. Among the more expensive toys are extremely complex robots. They are

RIGHT (MAIN PICTURE) *Gebrüder Märklin continued to make excellent large-scale models of warships well into the 1920s. This example is powered by electricity and has three propellers and a hoist for lowering a seaplane onto the water.*

RIGHT (INSET) *This unusual motorcycle delivery vehicle is unmarked but has the appearance of an Italian toy. Dating to the late 1930s, it has bright nickle plating and the clockwork motor, housed in the engine section, has a belt drive to the rear wheels.*

among the most inventive of all modern tinplate toys and are attracting progressively higher prices as they develop a wide following. At present, the most passionate collectors of robots are Japanese, but the appeal of robots is becoming more international and they are beginning to appear in toy auctions and specialist exhibitions.

UNDERSTANDING THE MARKET

WHEN PURCHASING RECENT tinplate such as robots or aircraft, it is advisable to make sure that they are still in working order, as much of their appeal depends on their complete perform-ance with lights, sound and movement. It often surprises non-specialists to discover that collectors of vintage tinplate are unconcerned as to whether a toy is in full working order. To the enthusiast, a motor car with good, original paintwork and fine external condition is preferable by far to one that runs beautifully but is badly chipped or dented.

For anyone beginning to collect metal toys, it is essential to be made aware of any repairs or replacement parts. Recently, because of the great skill of some restorers, it has become fashionable for dealers to claim that a re-paint by a highly regarded restorer is almost as good as an original finish — a claim that is obviously untrue, since nothing can compare with the soft patina of age. While it is proper to restore a toy that has lost almost all of its original paintwork, this course should be a last resort; originality is always preferable.

Replacement parts in non-ferrous metals or even plastic substances are also common, and the new collector needs to

ABOVE As the footballers run along, the ball, which houses the clockwork motor, swings from side to side. Marked 'Made in the US Zone of Germany', the toy dates to the 1950s.

RIGHT Made by Johann Distler c1925, this limousine, complete with chauffeur, was intended for a cheap market.

OPPOSITE This fantasy American racing car, made in America by Marx in the 1930s, is gaudily lithographed,

examine all sections of an expensive toy with great care before purchase. Most reputable dealers will supply buyers with a detailed bill stating condition, age and manufacturer. Those hunting in street markets, car boot or garage sales are completely on their own and it is there that highly priced fakes and 'marriages' are most likely to be encountered. What might seem to be the bargain of all time often turns out to be a clever mock-up, using parts from different periods and even from completely different vehicles. Established dealers, collectors' clubs and some auction rooms are all willing to assist new collectors who want to buy sensibly as an investment. They are aware that expensive mistakes can put people off collecting. So it is in their interest to give a degree of protection until the buyer has confidence in his own judgement.

Many antique toys are now purchased from mailing lists or auction catalogues, in which some general terms are used to describe condition. 'Very good' indicates that the piece is without any blemishes or dents, though it might be slightly faded or have the patina of age. 'Good' means that the piece is

in reasonable, but not superb, condition. 'Play-worn' is an all-embracing term that can include anything from a slightly chipped toy to one that has lost all its paint and some parts as well! The latter category is more suitable for the restorer or a collector seeking spare parts to repair another item. As restoration can be very expensive, it is better for the novice to avoid items in very bad condition; they are very difficult to re-sell and repairs can cost more than the price of a perfect example. The phrase 'mint and boxed' is occasionally used for tin toys, but is more often reserved for die-cast models of a more recent date. Perfection is necessary before a piece can legitimately be so described.

If a toy is purchased with some documentation, such as original receipts or a photograph of it with the first owner, these should be safely stored. Original boxes, even if in very poor condition, should also be kept, since they often help to establish the date or manufacturer. Toys in attractive boxes, such as those used by Lehmann or Martin, are especially desirable and the original packaging adds to the value.

RIGHT *This novelty toy, a 'sand-scoop', was made by Bing Werke c1925. As the small black handle is turned, a belt drives the large wheel, causing the arm to scoop sand from the bottom tray and drop it onto the slope on the left which returns it to the tray.*

OPPOSITE TOP *A fine steam-powered model of a fire-engine, made by Gebrüder Bing c1905. The spirit-fired copper boiler has a water level gauge.*

OPPOSITE BOTTOM *A spirit-fired, live-steam road roller by Gebrüder Bing. The single cylinder drives a fly-wheel to maintain momentum. Hand-painted, it is based on German prototypes seldom seen in other countries.*

MAINTENANCE

IN ORDER TO keep the toys in good condition, they should be stored in an area where the temperature is constant. Rapid changes of temperature, producing expansion and contraction, can damage the surface of painted or lithographed tinplate. Humidity is also a great problem, as a damp environment can give rise to that great horror of metal-toy collectors, rust. This is by far the worst hazard because once the rusting process has begun it is very difficult to halt, and the oxidization will damage the paint.

If toys are displayed in a living room, it is advisable to protect them from dust in glass-fronted cases in which sachets of moisture-absorbent substances can be hidden. As sunlight will fade paintwork, the pieces should be kept in the darkest part of the room. Muslin curtains that filter damaging ultraviolet rays can also be used, though these need to be of the museum-approved type. Even comparatively cheap toys deserve protection, as every true collector works to avoid any deterioration while an object is in his care.

All toys require occasional dusting and this should be done with a very soft cloth or paint brush. It is not advisable to use any cleaning substances or soap and water. The former will gradually scratch the surface and the latter will cause rust. If a toy is very dirty, wipe it gently with a little machine oil applied with a soft cloth. It can take a long time to clean the surface, but this is the only way to be sure that no damage is being caused. It is a great temptation to polish or wax a toy once it is clean but this too should be resisted as a little of the polish will always remain on the surface and eventually alter the appearance. An antique toy should not look as though it has just left the factory. If it does, it has probably been over-cleaned or over-restored.

If a toy has any flaking paintwork, it should not be touched at all as it could easily be ruined. Almost any damage is best ignored if there is any possibility that you might want to sell the toy. Most advanced collectors prefer to supervise the restoration themselves. Non-operational mechanisms should also be ignored, as attempts to repair clockwork motors often result in the breaking of the metal joining tabs or damage to paintwork. Most collectors prefer a non-working toy to one that has been mended by an amateur. The soldering iron is even more dangerous than rust, as its heat often damages paint. It is better to use glue to hold part together, though even this has to be used with great care as some types will damage paint.

MODEL RAILWAYS

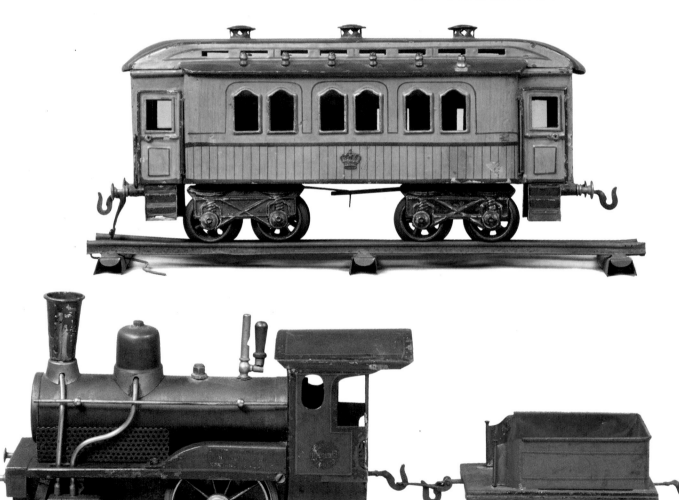

RAILWAYS, AS A form of transport, captured the imagination of the public powerfully and immediately. At first, people were frightened by dire warnings of the severe damage that the human frame would suffer when subjected to speeds in excess of 30mph (48kph). But quite quickly the romance of the train overcame fright, and the continuing love affair with railway engines began.

Inevitably, in the golden days of the tin-toy manufacturers before World War I, many superb models were produced in the great factories of Nuremberg and Göppingen, but although these form the centrepiece of any serious collection of model railways, they were by no means the first.

The opening of the Stockport to Darlington railway in 1825 led to the great rush of building across the world, and the major events were celebrated by many of the traditional toymakers. Among the earliest is a representation of the first train on the Nuremberg to Fürth line, made as a flat figure, in the manner of the early lead soldiers. It shows an engine pulling a tender and two stage-coach-type carriages, with a guard sitting on the roof of the last. Dating from 1835, it is in the tradition of the pleasure gardens and zoos that appeared

from the Regency period onwards, and was more a decorative than a practical toy.

The makers of wooden toys also sold representations of trains, some complete with wooden rails, and while these are crude, they give some idea of the style of engines and rolling stock of the period. More realistic were the early scale models, mainly produced by the makers of scientific instruments, that often served as selling aids, or as prototypes before production in full scale. These are so rare and fine that they are out of the reach of the ordinary collector.

CLOCKWORK AND STEAM MODELS

IT WAS NOT until the second half of the 19th century that the production of model railways began in earnest, with toys that ran either by clockwork or live steam. Oddly, many of these were retrospective in design, representing prototypes that had been obsolete for up to 30 years, perhaps pandering to fathers with fond memories of their own childhood.

The simplest of the clockwork models held a motor in a central box, and the train was drawn in a circle by means of a

OPPOSITE *A gauge 1 coach from the Kaiser Train, the royal train of Germany, made by Gebrüder Bing c1902. The clerestory roof opens to reveal tables and chairs. By the same maker, but dating to c1895 is the gauge 1 2-2-0 locomotive and tender.*

RIGHT *Also by Gebrüder Bing is this gauge 1 Compagnie Internationale des Wagon-Lits sleeping car, which is hand painted except for the transfer-printed gold lettering.*

long arm of wire. Known as the Rotary Railway Express, this is one of the first tinplate model train sets. Small in size, it was only 1⅞in (4.4cm) high and the engine, tender and two carriages a total of 12in (30cm) long. Similar small tinplate trains, not intended to run on tracks, were made, particularly in France, which was at the time more successful than Germany in production of metal toys. Most of them were without any form of motive power, and were simple push toys.

The earliest toy engines were mainly steam powered floor runners — not designed to run on tracks — and, because of their propensity for leaking water from their valve gear, they were known as 'Birmingham dribblers' or 'Piddlers'. Most had the front, non-driving wheels set at an angle, so that the engine would always run in a circle. These little engines, fired by methylated spirit-burners, must have been an immense fire risk, as they were prone to turn over!

The British and the French were among the most prominent makers of this type of engine and firms such as Stevens Model Dockyard of London and the Clyde Model Dockyard of Glasgow were particularly well known in the field. Neither appears to have been a very large concern, and while their advertisements proudly proclaim the products as 'Our Own Make', there is strong evidence that most of the smaller manufacturers bought in parts, or indeed complete models, from each other. One of the sources of such supply was the Paris-based firm of Radiguet et Massiot, whose products may easily be identified in the catalogue produced by the Clyde Model Dockyard.

Most of the early companies would supply either the completed engine, ready to fire, or a kit of parts for home assembly. While, as always, the more expensive the model, the greater the degree of realism and the better the finish, it should not be thought that these toys were in any sense true scale models; they were merely reasonable representations of the prototypes. Nor was there, in the early days, any attempt

LEFT *A very fine gauge 1 model of the Great Western Railway 4-6-2 locomotive* The Great Bear *with its twin bogie tender. Powered by live steam, it is a reasonably accurate representation of its prototype.*

to standardize gauges — manufacturers simply used what seemed reasonable for the size of the model.

Engines are classified by the number of wheels, both in full-size and in models. The first number indicates how many leading wheels there are, the second the number of driving wheels and the third the number of trailing wheels. Thus a 2-4-0 engine has two leading, four driving and no trailing wheels. Very rarely on toys an additional set of driving wheels is encountered, and the configuration is then written, for example, 0-6-6-0. Most of the late-Victorian engines in Europe were in fact of the 2-2-0 type, the leading wheels being strikingly small and because of their appearance known as 'stork-legs'.

Not all of the early models were crude. Newton and Co., of London, turned out excellent examples, made almost entirely of unpainted brass, with ebony being used for the buffer beams. Newtons were primarily scientific instrument makers, producing models only to special order, and their work is much finer than that normally found in the products of the model dockyards.

Another British instrument maker who produced exceptionally fine models was H.J. Wood, father of the conductor, Sir Henry Wood. The quality of his work varied greatly, presumably in accordance with the amount of money that his clients wished to spend, but his best models do qualify as true scale models, not simply toys.

It was only at the end of the 19th century that the revolution in model railway occurred that was to make them truly accessible to a wide public. At the Spring Fair in Leipzig in 1891, the Märklin company showed for the first time trains running on a standard system of gauges, from 1 to 4.

The size of the railway system, whether in full scale or miniature, is expressed in terms of the width of the tracks, which in Germany was measured until 1930 from the centre of the railheads; since that date, by international agreement, it has been measured from the inside edge of the rails, a difference in model railway of around $\frac{1}{8}$in (3mm). Confusion is added by the fact that, for a long time, there was no agreement among manufacturers as to which gauge corresponded to a given number: thus Bing's gauge 4 is the same size as Märklin's gauge 3. When smaller sizes were later introduced, the gauge below 1 logically was called '0', and even later the half gauge '00' or 'H0'. Further miniaturization destroyed the earlier numerical pattern, and the smallest size now available is called 'N'.

The trains of the late 19th century, even those made by the major manufacturers, are almost surprisingly crude, with the clockwork versions being little more than primitive sketches

BELOW *Jean Schoenner made very fine large-scale models of trains in Germany. This gauge 3 live-steam 4-4-0 is based on a P.L.M. Coupe Vent. Made c1900, it takes its name from the shaping of the funnel and the front of the boiler.*

of the prototypes. The wheels look large and clumsy and the rolling stock is simply stamped from the tinplate and hand-painted; indeed the charm of these pieces lies in their very crudeness. They were, of course, intended chiefly for the lower middle classes, who had neither the space to house nor the money to buy the larger-scale steam-fired locomotives (which might cost as much as a poorer manual worker earned in a year).

Among the best, and most sought-after, of the late-19th-century German manufacturers was Jean Schoenner, whose factory in Nuremberg first opened in 1875. Schoenner's output remained fairly small, but he produced some of the most impressive engines in a mixture of pressed tinplate and brass. Perhaps the most remarkable was a large $5\frac{11}{16}$in (13.7cm) gauge model, the *Luitpold*, which was shown at the Paris Exhibition of 1900. The Bavarian State Railways 4-4-0

OPPOSITE TOP *No good railway layout was complete without a destination board, such as this good Märklin example made c1910. It displays a variety of romantic sounding Continental locations.*

OPPOSITE BOTTOM *A Hornby Dublo Royal Mail van. When the car passed a switch by the side of the track, the doors opened to collect a sack of mail.*

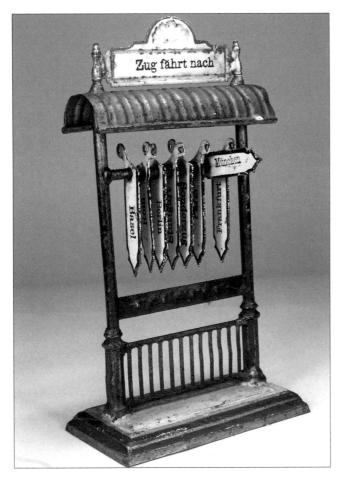

locomotive, which stands 16¼in (39cm) high and is 40in (98cm) long, is sufficiently large for a wealth of detail, and the work is finer than that found in the work of any other maker of the period. While this was obviously an special exhibition piece, Schoenner's more commercial examples, which were often sold in Great Britain through the Bassett-Lowke company, were also often extremely fine, and there are still some that, although known through catalogue drawings, have not yet appeared on the market.

Bassett-Lowke also retailed the products of other makers from Germany, particularly Georges Carette, the Nuremberg-based Frenchman. Carette was perhaps the first of the toymakers to produce models that were reasonably true to their prototypes. One of the earliest was the *Lady of the Lake*, an unusual 2-2-2 Great Northern Railways locomotive with a very large driving wheel. It appeared in the catalogues at the turn of the century. Because of the accuracy of the models and relatively short life of the company, Carette's pieces always command high prices.

The wealth of Great Britain led most of the major German toymakers to concentrate their marketing efforts on that country, although the United States, both as a selling area and a source of prototypes, was not ignored. American designs held an appeal on both sides of the Atlantic. The Bassett-Lowke catalogue of 1904, for example, shows a Carette model

of the Vaucan compound engine which ran on the New York Central railway and was, at the time, one of the most famous American locomotives. In common with most other models of the period, it was available with either clockwork or steam power. Its appeal to the British was that it was totally unlike the engines with which they were familiar, having such exotic accessories as cowcatchers.

Probably the most famous collaboration between Nuremberg and Great Britain was that between Bing and Bassett-Lowke. Stefan Bing met the English businessman at the 1900 Paris Exhibition, and shortly afterwards Bing engines and rolling stock were introduced into Bassett-Lowke's catalogue. One of the earliest, and most famous, results of this collaboration was the London and North Western Railway's 4-4-0 locomotive, the *Black Prince*. Bing's work was invariably higher in weight and less detailed than that of his main competitors, but the output of the factory was so great that examples of the firm's products are more easily available than any other, except perhaps Märklin.

By the turn of the century, and in the years preceding World War I, Märklin produced a large quantity of excellent models, based on prototypes from all over the world, which achieved wide international sales. Märklin did not compete with the best of the work of Jean Schoenner or Georges Carette, but the company pursued a consistent policy of excellence and realism that led it to dominate the world market and its early work still commands substantial prices. Throughout this early period, Märklin's major emphasis, in common with most other European manufacturers, was on gauge 1 or larger; gauge 0 did not really gain a hold until the inter-war years.

Railways could provide horrifying copy for the newspapers when accidents occurred, and there were several spectacular crashes at the beginning of the century. Children who enjoyed engineering such castrophes for themselves were assisted by Märklin, who brought out a complete train which disintegrated on impact. Springs threw the sides and roofs off carriages, and only mangled corpses were lacking for total realism.

Many smaller German firms produced interesting, and in some cases novel, trains. Karl Bub of Nuremberg, in addition to making many fairly unexceptional (but nevertheless collectable) trains, produced the *Whatsamatter*. After running a short distance, the train stops and the driver's head appears through a trap in the cab, as if to inspect an obstruction. Satisfied, he re-enters, and the train runs on to the next delay.

Small, crude trains were also produced by Hess, mainly in very small scale and either flywheel- or clockwork-powered, or indeed unpowered. These were brightly lithographed, as opposed to the handpainting that was common on the better toys, and were floor runners. Cheap and amusing, they were more in the nature of stocking fillers than serious models.

Ernst Planck of Nuremberg, a firm that specialized in scientific toys, such as projectors, magic lanterns and stationary engines, made a number of trains. Rather crude, both in scale and finish, they are characterized by coarse wide wheels with deep flanges. Interesting because of their rarity, they are prevented by their crudeness from attaining the high prices that more common, but better made, models of other makers reach.

In England, the early years were dominated by Bassett-Lowke, who imported most of their stock, but did have a manufacturing facility which supplied mainly larger-gauge, well-engineered models. The firm's output increased after World War I, when, despite the fact that Carette had ceased

OPPOSITE *A group of 0 gauge engines and accessories made by Märklin during the 1930s. At the top is the* Hamburg Flyer. *In the centre is the* Der Adler, *made to commemorate the centenary of the opening of the first German railway in 1835, and the electrically powered Southern Railway 4-4-0* Merchant Tailors.

LEFT *The unusual Great Northern Railway 4-2-2* Lady of the Lake *features large driving wheels. One of the earlier realistic interpretations of actual prototypes, it was made by Georges Carette of Nuremberg.*

BELOW *Early models were often crude and simple, especially when intended for the cheaper end of the market. This train set, in approximately 00 gauge, was made c1910 by Gebrüder Bing.*

production in 1917, Bassett-Lowke mysteriously obtained many of that firm's dies and were thus able to continue to make models previously supplied from Germany. Similarly, after the Bing family lost control of their company and fled Nazi Germany, Bassett-Lowke assisted them in the setting up of the English Trix company, which produced smaller-gauge model railways.

After World War I, many people felt that it was unpatriotic to buy German toys. A gap opened in the market, and to fill it, Hornby, which had previously made only the Meccano construction kits, began to produce train sets. The early products were 0 gauge, and some excellent models, such as the 4-6-2 *Princess Elizabeth*, appeared. Hornby quickly achieved a position of market dominance in the United Kingdom, so that their name became almost synonymous with model railways. They also made an early entry into the European market, establishing their French-manufacturing facility before the outbreak of World War II. Their range was wide, from simple, cheap, clockwork-powered tank engines to sophisticated and reasonably accurate representations of mainline express locomotives, such as the Midland Railway's *Princess Elizabeth*, powered by electricity, which was made from 1937 to 1939.

OPPOSITE *The Paris firm of Charles Rossignol specialized in making flimsy but attractive toys, such as this 0-6-0 clockwork floor runner. Originally bright, the finish has aged.*

THE AGE OF ELECTRICITY

ALTHOUGH ELECTRIC POWER was used as early as 1880 by Ernst Planck, who exhibited the system at the 1882 Bavarian Trades Exhibition, no examples from this early date have so far been found. Among the earliest commercial producers of model electric trains was the American firm of Voltamp, which was marketing them from about 1890. In Europe they did not become available until some 10 years later, when all the major manufacturers were almost forced to offer electricity as an alternative to clockwork and steam. Because of the difficulty in producing a satisfactory transformer to convert high-voltage alternating current to low-voltage direct, as well as stringent government regulations, the method did not become generally accepted in Britain until the 1920s.

The smaller houses built after World War I forced the makers of model railways to re-assess the market. Bassett-Lowke was again in the lead, persuading Bing to produce the first 'Table Top Railway', half the size of 0 gauge and known as either 'H0' or '00'. This eventually became almost the standard, and few manufacturers now produce models above this size.

In the United States, the market was served at an early date by native manufacturers, who worked mainly in gauge 1 or larger. One of the first was Eugene Beggs of New Jersey, who in 1875 obtained a patent for a model engine made of cast iron. To compensate for this increased weight, his rolling stock had cardboard bodies, covered with lithographed paper. These colourful, but inherently fragile, toys are now avidly collected, but are in very short supply. The firm did not have a long life, ceasing production in 1906.

Tinplate toys were made in Forestville, Connecticut, a centre of the clockmaking industry, and the first American tinplate engines were made there by George W. Brown who, in common with European manufacturers, produced many toys other than railways. By the 1870s there was a fairly large-

OPPOSITE *The Hornby Dublo system immediately recognized the developments in railway transport. This British Railway diesel locomotive, made partly of plastic, dates to the late 1950s.*

ABOVE *The realism of the British-made Hornby Dublo locomotives and rolling stock was achieved by the use of die-casting. This 0-6-0 tank engine dates to the 1950s and is a British Railways goods engine.*

scale production, and although some models were clock-work-powered, the majority were simple push-alongs, and almost all were floor runners.

The most famous name in American model railway history is that of Edward R. Ives, who established his business in Plymouth, Connecticut, in 1868, moving two years later to Bridgeport. The company slogan, 'Ives Toys make Happy Boys', featured prominently in their advertisements. For a period the company held in the United States the market dominance that Hornby had in Great Britain, but Ives was an early victim of the Depression, running into financial difficulties which led to bankruptcy in 1928. Ives produced a wide variety of trains, from early tinplate and cast iron floor runners to steam-powered cast iron. In 1910 the company produced the first '0' gauge electric system in the United States.

Although the name of Ives continued for a time after the bankruptcy, by 1933 the company had been absorbed by Lionel, which had been founded in New York in 1906 and had

ABOVE *Makers in all countries produced rolling stock compatible to the countries of sale. This luggage car, for the New York Central Railway, includes a section for the guard with a desk and chair, as well as a kitchen with a dresser and stove. The gauge 1 car was made by Bing Werke c1925.*

pursued its own distinctive style, even to the extent of using a non-standard size. Slightly larger than normal gauge 2 at $2\frac{1}{10}$in (54mm), it was promoted as the 'American Standard Gauge'. An advantage to the company was that only its rolling stock and accessories could run on the system, ensuring brand loyalty once the first purchase had been made. Larger than most of its competitors, a Lionel train of the 1930s, with streamlined bodywork and silver paint, is a stylish evocation of the great US railway era.

The third giant of the US scene was American Flyer, which also started operations at the beginning of the century. Its major emphasis was on 0 gauge, and the range of its products is wide, almost entirely based on United States prototypes, although there was a short-lived attempt during the 1920s to break into the English market with a clockwork-powered, cast-iron engine. For its domestic market, the company mainly produced electric-powered trains and its models are rarely found in Europe.

OPPOSITE *A simple 0 gauge King George V made c1912 by Gebrüder Bing. The 2-4-0 locomotive, though very sturdily made, lacks the fine detail of larger models.*

ROLLING STOCK
AND ACCESSORIES

INEVITABLY, COLLECTORS PLACE most emphasis on the locomotives, but much of the attraction of a railway setting is in the rolling stock: here, the variety is greater than in the engines themselves. From the very beginning, manufacturers have provided all the necessary accessories to complete the trains — passenger carriages, goods wagons, guard vans and even mobile cranes.

The earliest commercial models of rolling stock were mainly passenger coaches, and, like the engines, they were relatively crude, simply stamped from tinplate and hand painted in the appropriate livery, with the windows left as empty spaces. As the sets became more sophisticated, so did the carriages. By the early years of the 20th century, a bewildering array, with good detail, could be found. They were still rather untrue to the originals, but were better than the mere

sketches that had been provided at first. Particularly interesting are the coaches based on continental prototypes, such as the 'Swiss gallery carriage', which has an observation platform running the length of the carriage, the guard rails ornamented with Gothic tracery and heavy mouldings to the pillars supporting the roof. Produced by Märklin from 1909 to 1920, it has opening doors leading to the compartments. Passengers could be purchased separately to complete the scene.

The search for increasing realism led to the introduction of coaches with opening doors, windows glazed with mica and seats in the compartments. So that the passengers might sit neatly when the train was in motion, Märklin and Bing soldered pins on to the seats, and the composition figures had corresponding holes into which the pins fitted. Carette passengers, however, had the pin fitted to them, which slotted into a hole in the seat — a ready means of identifying some unmarked figures or coaches.

With the introduction of lithography, the presentation of the same basic body in different guises became easier, and dining cars, sleeping cars and Pullman carriages became more commonly available. Many of the manufacturers supplied department stores under contract with sets which were sometimes marked only with the store's name. Märklin, for example, was a regular supplier to Gamages of London, and the make of these models is mainly identified by reference to known and marked models sold through other sources. The finest detail was on the larger-gauge models; with the introduction of the smaller 00, the surface became more important than the interior.

It would be almost impossible for a collector to obtain a complete set of all the goods wagons made by one manufacturer, for the range of service vehicles was even greater than that of passenger coaches. As each advance was made, it was recognized by the toymakers. Thus, when the British used armoured trains in the Boer War, Märklin reproduced them in miniature. With the advent of the motor car, the distribution of fuel became important and was mainly undertaken by rail: tanker wagons, decorated with company logos, such as those of Shell or Anglo-American Oil, were quickly introduced into the catalogues. Coal trucks and timber wagons, complete with twigs for tree trunks, became a commonplace

in the toy cupboard, especially as goods vehicles were cheaper than passenger carriages. More easily found, they are now consequently less expensive in the collector's market.

Unusual and rare items obviously command the highest prices. In Great Britain, the Colman's Mustard truck, painted in the distinctive bright yellow and decorated with the royal coat of arms, is at a premium because of its scarcity, especially the gauge 1 version produced by Carette. Märklin recognized the beginning of the trend towards containerization as early as 1910 and produced flat-bed wagons on which the containers were loaded. These are also rare and consequently expensive to purchase.

No layout was complete without the appropriate station buildings, and in this area the toymakers excelled themselves. Little effort was made to recognize styles of architecture other than that found in Germany, but the buildings are impressive examples of the tin workers' skill. Frequently the brickwork and tiles were impressed in the metal; and with windows, shutters, ticket collector's gates, waiting rooms and ticket offices, they remain charming examples of the Bavarians' ability to create exciting and attractive toys. The platform scenes were completed with passengers, railway staff, newspaper stands, benches and even cafés. Working oil lamps

could be used to light the scene, while there were signals, level crossing gates and tunnels to provide excitement and realism to the layout. All of these items command respectable prices, especially those made before World War I, for they provide the necessary background to the trains themselves.

With all this realism available to the collector, it is surprising that the track itself is of little or no value. This is partly because it is in abundant supply, but chiefly because the engines are now far too valuable to be used: steaming an early engine risks damage to the paintwork. Restoration always decreases the value, as does disfiguring wear-and-tear. Steam engines are especially susceptible to damage, as the heat of the boiler scorches the paint, while neglecting to drain the boiler results in corrosion. Even clockwork engines are seldom operated, to prevent possible damage to the spring. If they are wound up, care should be taken not to wind the motor fully, in order to prevent excessive pressure, which can cause the metal to snap.

MAINTENANCE

WHEN CARING FOR railway items, as dry an environment as possible is needed to prevent the onset of rust, which can be caused by excessive humidity. Cleaning must never be done with an abrasive substance, however mild, but with an oily, soft cloth. Moving parts sometimes benefit from the application of a light machine oil, but care must be taken to wipe off any surplus. Even if a piece is worn, it is never wise for anyone other than an expert to attempt restoration, for unless the right components and paints are used, the value of the piece is lost.

Railways have always been an important part of a boy's childhood, and they fascinate some men throughout their lives. The trains made for boys in the early part of this century, like their full-scale prototypes, have now earned an honourable retirement — providing enjoyment by the artistry of their workmanship rather than the excitement of their operation.

TOY SOLDIERS

PRIGHT YOUNG MEN in gorgeous uniforms, well-fed and groomed horses, fairy-tale forts and immaculate army vehicles — all present a picture of military life that was very far from the reality of war. When every boy played with toy soldiers, life in the army must have represented excitement and the romance of dressing up in splendid eye-catching uniforms for deeds of valour. In Germany, where military service was compulsory in the 19th century, the uniforms were especially striking and must have offered a young man some compensation for a period spent away from career and home.

Throughout their history, model soldiers have appealed to adults as well as children and expensive versions in precious metals and precise detail have been made alongside cheap, mass-produced examples. As so many figures have survived in good condition, soldiers form one of the most active collecting areas, with their own specialist groups: those who collect antique figures in near-perfect condition for display and those who use the models for their war games and accept examples in different materials, adaptations and re-paints.

As the value of soldiers in original condition has increased, collectors treat their acquisitions with great respect and there has been a marked decrease in the amount of repairing and re-modelling work done to them. The importance of original packaging is also respected, as the additional value of a boxed set is generally recognized. It was once quite common for respected collectors to remove complete sets for their war games and forget where they had put the boxes. Sad tales of auction room staff desperately trying to marry boxes and figures without success abound, especially in the area of executors' sales.

Toy soldiers were commercially made from a number of materials, including wood and composition, but those made of metal are the most avidly collected. The greatest amount of work was lavished on large figures that are almost doll-like in form and can stand up to 12in (30cm) high. Soldiers of this type, often dressed in actual fabrics from contemporary uniforms, have been made since the 16th century, though the majority that appear on the market were made after 1800. In general, this is a neglected area of soldier-collecting, despite the fact that the toys — sometimes with swords, guns and equipment — are fascinating historical documents.

OPPOSITE *One of the earliest methods of mass-producing soldiers was by turning. This group, made in the Erzgebirge region of Germany c1880, shows how simple added detail could give variety.*

RIGHT *An early 'Display Box' set by William Britain of five regiments of the British cavalry. They are the 11th Hussars, the 2nd Life Guards, the 12th Lancers, the Royal Scots Greys and the 1st Dragoons.*

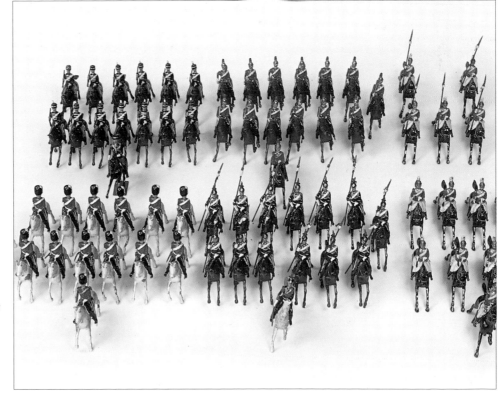

ABOVE *Grand Admiral Raeder and General von Blomberg, made by Elastolin in the late 1930s. A complete range of important military and political figures was made by this German firm.*

RIGHT *The Scots Guards set made by William Britain c1900. The figures have moveable arms and include a pipe major, an officer and six privates. The box lid lists the regiment's battle honours.*

TOY SOLDIER 'FLATS'

METAL WAS BY far the best substance for the representation of men in action, as the figures could be moulded in detail and given a base on which to stand. Once a standard scale for military figures was agreed upon, it became possible for soldiers from several sources to be grouped together for war games. As all the makers created models in the uniforms of many countries, the range of subject matter was vast and almost any battle could be re-enacted on the nursery floor.

The earliest commercially made metal soldiers were the 'flats' – in effect, outlines with embossed detail. They were made of very soft metal that is easily bent or broken and so require care in handling. 'Semi-flats' or 'half-rounds' are somewhat more realistic, but lack the intricate detail and painting seen on the flats. In the late 19th century hollow-casting made it possible to create figures in the round with realistic uniforms and equipment and delicate prancing horses. It is models of this type that are now most widely col-

ABOVE Very fine painted detail was lavished on the so-called 'flats'. This set of mid-19th-century Germany cavalry was modelled with great skill.

lected, especially those made by William Britain, the British firm that emphasised correctness of costume.

Though the hollow-casts made by British now attract the highest prices, the large flats made by German firms such as Hilpert reveal more artistry in their skilful colouring and intricate detail. The earliest recorded German metal soldiers date from the 13th century and commercial production began in 1578, when the Council of Nuremberg allowed pewterers to make tin figures as children's toys. It is thought that the designs for the first soldiers were based on military men represented in woodcuts. By the end of the 17th century there were special sheets of prints showing the uniforms of soldiers who fought in specific campaigns and these provided craftsmen, sometimes working in remote areas, with excellent detail.

Two-part moulds for the flats were made from slate, stone or wood, though the French maker, Mignot, used bronze. The general detail of the figure was gouged out and then the fine detail incised with delicate etching tools. A pouring channel was also cut out and pegs linked the two sides of the mould together. Molten metal, made to the manufacturer's secret formula, was then poured into the pre-heated mould. As pure tin disintegrates and is very brittle, some 40 per cent of lead, as well as some antimony and bismuth, was added.

Collectable flats are today valued according to the quality of the engraved detail, the verve of the outline and the skill of the painter. Some of the figures are minor works of art, with great character and presence; others are stiff and prosaic. As in all areas of soldier-collecting, boxed sets are preferred;

those containing flats are especially prized, because they are decorated with the medals won at various exhibitions.

The first great makers of tin flats were the Hilpert family (1720-1822), best known for a series of finely detailed monkeys and classical figures. Like most of the soldier-makers, the Hilperts made ornamental pieces for adults, including beautiful chess sets. Some of the toy scenes, such as a boar hunt or a portrait of Frederick the Great on horseback, are so well executed that they are now classed as pieces of folk art. Their regiments of soldiers were exported as far afield as the United States and remain the aristocrats of the genre.

German production of tin flats reached its peak in the mid-19th century, though there were small factories in Great Britain, Denmark, France and Switzerland and the United States. The Napoleonic wars had inspired a spate of table-top battles in the nurseries of Europe and the toy manufacturers were delighted to turn out colourfully dressed combatants by the thousand. The most prolific of the German makers was Ernst Heinrichsen who, in c1850, decided to concentrate on a 30mm size. It is now accepted as the 'Nuremberg Scale'. Heinrichsen depicted battles from all periods, including classical antiquity, the Crusades and the Crimean war. Ernst Wilhelm was the last of the Heinrichsen family and died in 1938.

Apart from the famous Hilperts and Heinrichsens, there were many other makers of flats based in Berlin, Gotha,

BELOW *The Bahamas Police Band, made by William Britain after World War II, is very rare and achieves high prices in the salerooms.*

LEFT *Regiments from all parts of the Empire were made by William Britain. This set of the 1st Bombay Lancers, which includes seven troopers with lances and two officers with swords, dates to the late 1800s.*

Luneberg, Diessen and Potsdam. Unfortunately the soldiers are not marked and have to be valued purely on appearance. A few of the original boxes carry the maker's name, but most simply show a series of medals. The soldiers were originally sold by weight rather than number and the smallest box was the 4oz size. Some of the large, boxed gift sets containing figures for a complete battle were sold together with maps or instructions.

One of the few German firms still producing flats is Babette Schweitzer, a concern that creates both decorative and toy items for export all over the world. Other smaller makers produce soldiers and scenes in limited numbers for the collectors' market. There is also some production of unpainted figures.

HOLLOW-CAST AND SEMI-SOLID MODELS

IT IS THOUGHT that the first semi-solid and solid soldiers originated in Germany, where Georg Heyde of Dresden was the most famous maker. Heyde began production in *c*1840 and concentrated mainly on boxed battle and parade sets. The firm's models were made in several sections so that they could be adapted according to demand. The heads were plugged in place and the riders fixed to their saddles with pegs. Battle scenes, classical groups, American Indians and all the regiments of Europe were made in different sizes, either as semi-solids or hollow-cast. Before 1900 most British and American children played with soldiers produced by Heyde, but their

BELOW *Any boxed set always attracts interest but this Band of the US Marines, made by William Britain, is especially desirable as the figures have never been taken out.*

lack of complete realism lost the battle for sales after 1900.

French toy-soldier manufacture was never so important as that of Germany, though some fine models were made, especially by Lucotte, which began production in the late 18th century. Later marked Lucotte figures carry the initials 'LC' together with the Imperial bee. Their models were eventually taken over by the much larger firm of Mignot, that began manufacture in *c.* 1825. Their mark, 'CBG' is made up of the initials of Cuperly, Blondel and Gerbeau, the three founders. The soldiers by Mignot stand 2-2½in (5-6cm) high and are mainly based on the French army. The finest are superb models, made to the highest specifications, with refinements such as soldiers that can be removed from their horses.

Mignot worked from the same Parisian workshops until the 1980s, when 14 workmen were employed in the manufacture of hand-made figures. During its 150 years of production, CBG Mignot assembled a stock of some 3,000 moulds for round and half-round figures, and 800 moulds for flats. In addition they acquired models from Lucotte. Their 1983 catalogue showed figures from French military history, including the Algerian war of independence, World War I and the Egyptian campaign of Napoleon. They always produced a number of expensive boxed settings, such as a reception at Malmaison, while their scenes from the Gallic wars show all

OPPOSITE TOP *A rare boxed set of the Royal Fusiliers made c1895 by William Britain. Such sets are seldom found with the original packaging intact.*

OPPOSITE BOTTOM *Not all model soldiers were represented in dress uniform. This mixed group of World War I and II soldiers by William Britain are all wearing khaki. This set also includes searchlights, aircraft listening posts and a first aid post.*

aspects of military life, including a Roman soldier pursuing a French lady, army kitchens, field hospitals and individual men cutting wood or cooking. To make the scenes more realistic, there are battering rams, scaling ladders and horse- and bullock-drawn provision wagons.

It was in Great Britain that the most realistic soldiers, meeting the demand from children and war games enthusiasts, emerged. British production of toys had never compared with that of Germany and France, but by the end of the 19th century some makers were making efforts to capture a larger part of the market. William Britain (1828-1906) was typical of this more progressive breed of businessman and made a variety of toys and window-display pieces that almost qualify as automata. His eldest son, who was interested in the various methods of creating model soldiers, devised a hollow-cast process that revolutionized production.

ABOVE *The Royal Horse Artillery dressed in khaki and wearing steel helmets is an unusual variant on the more normal full-dress version. Made by William Britain c1920, the set attracts strong interest among collectors.*

BELOW *Before World War I, William Britain made models of foreign armies. The Austro-Hungarian Army Lancers, pictured here, is, however, less specific than the firm's models of the British Army.*

The first Britain's soldiers appeared on the market in 1893 and the success of the venture was assured once Gamages, the London store that supplied toys by mail order all over the world, marketed them as 'English-made'. This was a useful selling ploy in the days of Empire and became increasingly so an anti-German feeling developed just before World War I.

Hollow-cast figures, being standard-sized, were ideal for war games: the men were always 54mm high with complementary horses and equipment. Accuracy of uniform was especially important, a feature that the colourful German soldiers had often lacked. Britain's soldiers were ideal for the nursery, cast from alloy and therefore relatively light. The first to be marketed were Life Guards with an officer and four troopers, quickly followed by subjects like the Boer Cavalry, the 5th Dragoon Guards and the Royal Fusiliers.

The characteristic bright red, almost lacquer-like, boxes that Britain used have excited recipients ever since they first appeared under Christmas trees and it is soldiers in the original packaging that are most coveted by collectors. The first special display boxes were sold from 1894 and were made up from four existing sets, which made them expensive. A reporter in *Athletic Sports, Games and Toys* (October, 1895) commented that the firm had already placed on the market more than 20 sets of soldiers from the regiments of the British army and that the Royal Horse Artillery, the Regimental Band of the Line and the Full Band of the Coldstream Guards were to be added to the list.

Britain's advertising literature claimed that the soldiers were produced entirely by British labour and that only innocuous paints and spirit varnish was used in their decoration. Some of the large presentation cases were very expensive and contained two inside trays for the display of as many as 275 pieces of cavalry and infantry. Alongside the basic soldier sets there were pieces such as the horse-drawn ambulance of the Royal Medical Corps. In addition to soldiers, there were railway scenes with passengers and luggage and football teams like Sheffield Wednesday and Aston Villa. There was even a model of the Football Association cup in silver or gilt.

ABOVE *Wooden toy infantry from a boxed set that includes an officer and a drummer. Made in the Erzebirge region of Germany in the 1870s.*

LEFT *A group of finely detailed flats representing German cavalry of the 1840s. They are of a type made in Germany throughout the 19th century, but are unattributable without their original boxes.*

modelled with rifles at the slope instead of 'at the trail' and this was corrected in subsequent issues. After World War II, an American colonel wrote to say that the lance heads of US Marine Forces were silver, not gold, and this was at once corrected. Since the company has continued to produce toys for such a long period, there is an abundance of material for the collectors' market and the price range is very wide. Worn or slightly damaged individual figures can still be purchased for next to nothing, while an 1893 set of the Royal Scots Greys, with plug shoulders and contained in the original box, could set you back some £3,000 ($5,000). Condition is extremely important, as the more sophisticated collectors require sets that are near-perfect in well-preserved boxes. Prices at the top end of the soldier market can be somewhat unpredictable. Occasionally a figure or a set will hit the headlines, yet a year later similar examples will sell for much less. This is usually because several sets appear on the market in the wake of publicity and it becomes evident that the toy is not so rare as originally believed.

Anyone beginning to collect model soldiers is advised to consult price guides and lists of auction realizations as well as specialist magazines; the proliferation of adapted and repainted figures can gull the uninitiated into making expensive mistakes. Some auction rooms hold sales devoted to soldiers and the catalogues carry estimates of the prices that are anticipated, estimates that help new collectors to avoid the more common pitfalls.

Foreign armies, such as the Japanese infantry, the Austro-Hungarian lancers and the United States infantry, were sold in attractive boxed sets. Red Indians, the German army, Arab horsemen, the Second Bombay Native Infantry and the Gurkha Rifles all appeared in the early years of production. The paper box labels that described the contents were individually designed for the same sets. Titles such as 'Dr Jameson and the African Mounted Infantry', the 'Turkish Infantry' and 'Africa's Savage Warriors, Zulus' all evoke the past and are collected by military as well as toy enthusiasts.

Britain's attention to accuracy was always paramount. In 1900 one customer complained that the rifle regiment was

OPPOSITE Both of the major makers of composition soldiers, Elastolin and Lineol, included Nazi figures in their ranges. The occupants of the car are by Elastolin and the standard-bearers by Lineol. The Fuhrerwagen was made by Tipp & Co.

ABOVE A Britain's set of the Royal Lancaster Regiment 'at the run', with a mounted officer, a bugler and a field gun.

LEFT Made in 1899, this set of Boer Infantry enabled children to re-enact the battles of that war. The original box adds greatly to the set's value and interest.

DIE-CAST TOYS

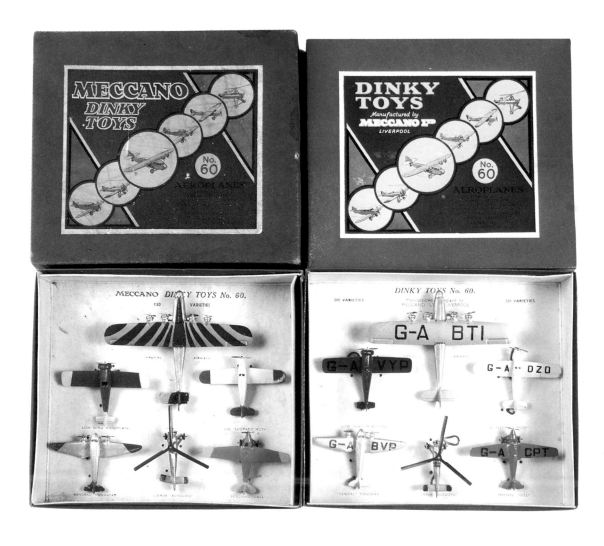

HE IMITATION OF transport in toy form reached its widest market with the introduction of the die-casting process, similar in concept to the method used by William Britain for the hollow-casting of soldiers. The earliest models were not, in fact, recognizable as particular types or makes of vehicle, but were merely generalized representations of cars or aeroplanes. Made of a soft lead alloy, they were quite well detailed, with delicate wheels. They appeared almost simultaneously in both France and the United States in *c*1910, being made by S.R. and Tootsietoy respectively. Small in size, they were about 2in (5cm) long, a scale that increased to a standard 3in (7.5cm) about five years later. In 1915 the first model based on an actual prototype was made. The 'Model T' Ford, probably the most famous car of its period, was then in its heyday, and a

toy version was marketed simultaneously by both S.R. and Tootsietoy in the new, larger size.

Although the majority of people associate die-casting methods almost exclusively with models of road transport, from the very beginning other toys, such as guns and aeroplanes, were made to the standard 2in (5cm) size. Detailed and attractive, they were far removed from full-sized objects that could fly or be fired with safety; rather they were visions of an improbable future, like the more recent space vehicles.

Being a cheap method of producing visually striking toys, die-casting attracted many of the major manufacturers, including Märklin, especially after the change of material from a lead to a zinc-based alloy, known as zamak or mazak, which also included magnesium, aluminium and copper. While mazak was lighter and harder than the lead alloy, it

RIGHT *One of the earliest sets of die-cast cars, made by Hornby c1938 to accompany their train sets before the name of Dinky was adopted. No effort was made during this perod to identify any specific vehicles.*

OPPOSITE *Two versions of the very rare, boxed sets of Dinky aeroplanes. The Meccano Dinky toy set is the earlier, but the later set is more realistic as it includes the aircraft registration letters.*

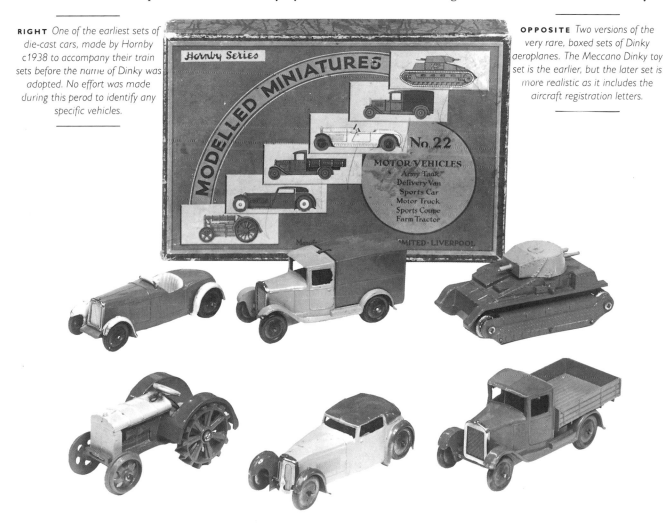

ABOVE *A fine group of mint-condition Dinky Supertoys of the early 1960s, shows varying bodies attached to the same chassis.*

tended, over a period, to become very brittle and to crack. This weakness, mainly caused by impurities in manufacture, is aggravated by humidity, and it can lead to the virtual destruction of a toy.

Being one of the first on the scene, Tootsietoy, a Chicago-based company, dominated the world market until the 1930s. Its range was vast, from aeroplanes and cars to cooking stoves to dolls' houses, and it worked mainly from American prototypes. The company was responsible for most of the technical innovations in production methods, introducing in 1928, for example, a separately cast radiator grille, nickel-plated for greater realism. It pioneered the use of mazak, and was the first to make a common chassis to which the bodies of different models were attached. From the mid-1920s Tootsietoy normally recessed the lines around doors and the engine compartment, while their European competitors continued to use unrealistic raised lines for another 30 years.

During the first third of the 20th century, die-cast toys in Great Britain were produced chiefly by the makers of soldiers, as adjuncts to their main business, and they provided

OPPOSITE *A boxed set of Tootsietoy die-casts made in the United States. The crudeness of the mould joints can clearly be seen and only generic types were made. Such boxed sets are extremely rare and command high prices.*

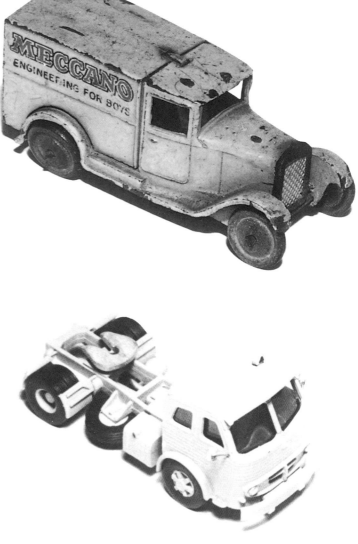

little serious threat to the imported Tootsietoys. In the early 1930s Hornby, which had largely captured the domestic model railway market, began to produce lead figures of people, to add realism to their layouts, and then went logically to the production of road vehicles in scale with their railways. Originally sold as 'Hornby Modelled Miniatures', the name was changed in 1934, first to 'Meccano Miniatures' and then to 'Meccano Dinky Toys'. Their success was immediate, partly because they were the product of an already successful company, but mainly because they were the first to be based on purely British prototypes.

Dinky retained its predominant position in the market in Great Britain until the late 1950s, although not without competition in the post-war years from Wells-Brimtoy, Mettoy and Chad Valley, all of which made die-casts as an addition to their tinplate ranges. One of the more interesting of the Chad Valley products was a range of models of Rootes Group vehicles. They were sold as promotional aids — in the manner of André Citröen — in Rootes garages as well as toyshops.

The company that eventually superseded Dinky as market leader was Lesney, founded in 1947. Originally it produced castings for other companies, but in the early 1950s it began to make its own models under the Matchbox label. By 1960 it was the strongest of the British manufacturers in the home market, and had achieved a similar position in the United

States, producing 75 new models a year. Of a smaller size than their predecessors (reverting to the 2in (5cm) standard), they captured the imagination of children with their representations of both current and early prototypes. So successful were they that the size again became an industry standard.

In 1956, Lesney's 'Models of Yesteryear' made their appearance prompted by the already burgeoning interest in the nostalgic. Priced identically to other toys in the range, they appealed to both children and adults, and were the first to create, almost accidentally, a new market for toys for the collector, which has continued to grow until the present day. They were also the first of the die-cast toys to show a significant increase in value over the short term, and were probably instrumental in creating the interest in the collecting of die-casts in general.

Although Lesney had captured a large section of the market in the 1950s, Dinky retained a strong following because of the larger size of their models. In the same year that the 'Models of Yesteryear' were launched, however, an attack on Dinky's primacy in the larger scale was made by Mettoy's introduction of its Corgi range. The models were more up-to-date than Dinky's and were made more realistic by the inclusion of features such as treaded tyres, aluminium

OPPOSITE LEFT *A complete traffic jam of Dinky toys but with a few Lesney 'Models of Yesteryear'. All date to the 1950s or later.*

OPPOSITE TOP RIGHT AND ABOVE *Two Dinky delivery vans, made c1935, are differentiated by the transfers. Such vehicles are now rare and the type of transfer can cause a major variance in price.*

BELOW *The earliest of the die-cast toys made by Lesney was this miniature coronation coach. It is now a quite valuable toy that seldom appears on the market.*

OPPOSITE BOTTOM RIGHT *Die-casts are now specifically made for the collector, and this model of a Pegaso tractor is made in kit form for home assembly.*

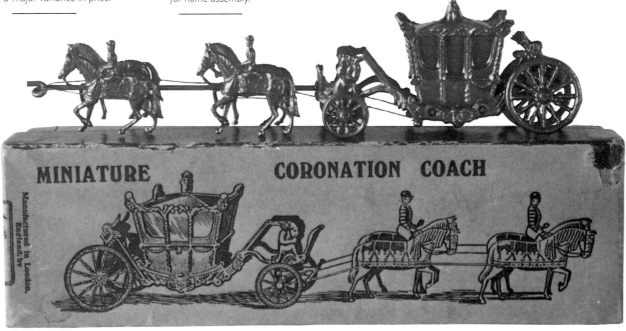

hub caps and plastic windows, something not previously seen on die-casts, but quite common on tinplate toys such as Triang's Minic series. The toys were well produced and made a severe impact on the dominance previously held by Hornby. Despite many vicissitudes, the Corgi name continues, and while the company aims mainly at the toy market, it produces a special range for collectors.

Triang, a firm that included in its catalogues almost every kind of toy, could not ignore die-casts. It entered the arena in 1959 with its own 'Spot-On' label. The venture was fairly short-lived, being abandoned in 1968, when Hornby, the makers of Dinky toys, was acquired. The 'Spot-On' toys had little impact on the market, as the models were, in the main, less well detailed than their rivals and lacked features that were becoming commonplace, such as opening doors and bonnets, which, although adding realism, weakened the structure.

ABOVE *Also rare and by the same maker is this model of an aeroplane. Such toys were not based on specific prototypes, and indeed such an aircraft could not possibly fly!*

BELOW *Three boxed sets of Dinky toys from the post-war period, based on World War II prototypes, and a large Britain's model of a howitzer, which ejected the shell-case after firing a projectile.*

OPPOSITE *A group of post-war Dinky toys. The military vehicles are now a collecting group on their own, while all the aircraft are of great interest, such as the Heinkel bomber at bottom left.*

During the 1960s, the British market was hit by an American range of small-scale cars, known as 'Hot Wheels'. Fitted with low-friction bearings and extremely thin axles, they were able to travel faster and further than other models, and all the other makers were forced to follow the trend, with names such as 'Superfast', 'Speedwheels' and 'Whizzwheels'. By this stage, the interior of the vehicles had become almost as important as the exterior, having such fittings as vacuum-moulded plastic seats and metal engine blocks.

European manufacturers made little effort at penetrating overseas markets, even though Märklin produced some die-casts and was, in fact, the first to use a tinplate base plate, on which the name of the model was stamped. The method was almost immediately followed by other manufacturers throughout the world. At its French factory Hornby produced a series of models based on French prototypes, as did Solido, which was the major force in that market.

The die-cast collector has a large choice of themes open to him, as most manufacturers tried to cover transport of every conceivable type. Some specialize in military models, which were among the earliest to be produced; others concentrate on individual manufacturers or models based on a particular prototype, such as the Jaguar car. There were also models associated with films, such as the James Bond series, or television, with the Thunderbirds. Large-scale sets of lorries and vans are also popular, and some of the good examples, such as Corgi's *Chipperfield Circus*, which included a Land Rover, crane, trailers and giraffes, are interesting and attractive toys that command substantial prices. In addition to road transport, there are aeroplanes, space vehicles and waterline models of ships, all of which have strong followings.

As with any toys, condition is of paramount importance, and in sales the highest prices are always paid for examples that can be called 'mint and boxed', although there is interest in items that are playworn if they are unusual models. The main enemies of die-casts are sunlight, which can lead to the fading of paint and applied logos, and excessive humidity, which can accelerate the onset of metal 'fatigue'. Some collectors attempt to overcome this by sealing all openings and joints with superglue, but this procedure is of doubtful value, since the decay, once started, is irreversible. There are now many spare parts available, especially tyres, for most models, and some collectors undertake quite extensive restoration, even though a restored vehicle does not command the same price as one in its original condition.

Because of the wide choice and the small size of the models, they have attracted a considerable following, and there are many specialized shows or 'swapmeets' for the devotees. Easy to display and inherently less fragile than tinplate, they are also much less expensive, and a good and interesting collection can be formed with little difficulty.

MAJOR PRODUCERS
OF METAL TOYS AND AUTOMATA

BASSETT-LOWKE – NORTHAMPTON, ENGLAND.

The company was established by Wenman J. Bassett-Lowke in 1898, although he had earlier made steam engines as part of his father's firm, J.T. Lowke & Son. The first retail shop was opened in 1908 and Bassett-Lowke was registered two years later in 1910. Märklin, Bing and Carette all supplied the firm. Although W.J. Bassett-Lowke died in 1953, the firm continued to make model railways until the late 1960s.

BING, GEBRÜDER – NUREMBERG, GERMANY.

Founded in 1863 by Ignaz and Adolf Bing, the firm made good quality tinplate toys. The mark 'G.B.N.' was used until 1919 when it was replaced by 'B.W.' (Bing Werke). The company closed down in 1934.

BONTEMS – PARIS.

Founded by Blaise Bontems in 1840, he was succeeded by his sons Charles and Alfred and by his grandson Lucien. Specialist automaton makers, the firm was especially known for its singing birds and tableaux.

BRIMTOY – LONDON.

The firm made tinplate toys from c1914, using Nelson's column as its trademark. It amalgamated with Wells in 1932 to form Wells Brimtoy.

BRITAINS – LONDON.

Established by William Britain in the late 1840s, William Britain Jnr created the first hollow-cast soldiers, marketed in 1893. Britains Ltd was incorporated in 1907. By 1965 they were producing plastic soldiers, but metal soliders reappeared in 1985.

BROWN, GEORGE W. – FORESTVILLE, CONNECTICUT, USA.

George W. Brown formed a clockmaking business in 1856, and was the first known toymaker in the US to use clockwork mechanisms. In 1869 the firm amalgamated with J. & E. Stephens to form Stephens and Brown Manufacturing Co., producing cast-iron toys and money boxes.

BUB, KARL – NUREMBERG, GERMANY.

Founded in 1851, the firm made tinplate toys and trains. In 1933 the company took over some of the Bing lines, and after World War II worked in conjunction with Tipp & Co., before closing in 1967.

CARETTE – NUREMBERG, GERMANY.

George Carette et Cie began producing tinplate toys in 1886, and supplied both Bing and to a larger extent Bassett-Lowke. The firm's peak period of production was between 1905 and 1914, but the factory closed in 1917 after Carette's return to his native France at the outbreak of war.

CHAD VALLEY – BIRMINGHAM, ENGLAND.

Established by Anthony Bunn Johnson before 1820, the name Chad Valley was used as a trademark from 1897, when their factory situated by the Chad stream was first opened. The firm made tinplate toys from this period until the mid 1950s.

CITROËN – FRANCE.

Founded by André Citroën as 'Les Jouets Citroën' in 1923 as a publicity promotion for their full-sized cars. After 1936 their toy cars were produced by 'C.I.J.' (Compagnie Industrielle du Jouet).

COX, JAMES – LONDON.

A clockmaker, jeweller and showman, James Cox (d 1788) also made automata, and he is best known for the *Silver Swan* in Bowes Museum, Co Durham, England.

CRESCENT TOY CO. – LONDON.

Founded in 1922, the firm produced hollow-cast figures.

DECAMPS – PARIS.

Established c1847, H.E. Decamps was the son-in-law of Jean Roullet, with whom he produced automata. 'R.D.' (Roullet et Decamps) was used as a mark. Gaston Decamps (1882-1972) continued the family tradition and produced some of the firm's best known work.

DISTLER – NUREMBERG, GERMANY.

The firm began producing tinplate toys in 1900, using a thistle and 'J.D.' as its mark. Eventually taken over by Trix, the company ceased production in 1962.

DROZ, PIERRE JAQUET – SWITZERLAND.

Droz (1721-1790) made clocks and automata with his son, Henri Louis Droz, and J.F. Leschot. His name sometimes appears engraved on the musical movement of his work.

EDISON, THOMAS – NEW JERSEY, USA.

Edison (1847-1931) patented the first phonograph doll in 1878. The commercially produced version, with a bisque head, was made from 1889.

ELASTOLIN – NEUSTADT, GERMANY.

The firm was founded in 1904 (Elastolin was the trade name), and specialized in composition figures that are marked 'Elastolin' on the base. It ceased production in the 1980s.

HAUSSER, O. & M. – LUDWIGSBERG, STUTTGARDT, GERMANY.

The founders of Elastolin, they had traded prior to 1904 as Muller & Freyer.

HEINRICHSEN, ERNST – NUREMBERG, GERMANY.

Founded in 1830, the firm specialized in metal soldiers. The firm was taken over by Ernst's son, Wilhelm, in 1869, and production eventually ceased in 1945.

HESS, MATH – NUREMBERG, GERMANY.

Founded in 1826, Hess was one of the first to make railways from pressed steel. Johann L. Hess inherited the company in 1866, and it ceased production in 1934.

HEYDE, GEORG – DRESDEN, GERMANY.

In production by 1870, the firm made soldiers of a solid and semi-solid type as well as a few hollow casts. The lids of their boxes carry details of the medals awarded the firm. Production ceased during World War II.

HILPERT – COBURG AND NUREMBERG, GERMANY.

In production from c1720-1822, succeeding generations of the Hilpert family made 'flat' figures, marked on their bases with 'H', 'Hilpert' or 'J.C. Hilpert'. The company is thought to have been one of the first to produce model armies made up of a large number of figures.

HORNBY, FRANK – LIVERPOOL, ENGLAND.

Hornby trains first appeared in 1920; electric trains were introduced in 1925 and in 1938 00 gauge trains (known as Hornby Dublo) were introduced. The firm began to market Dinky toys in 1933.

IVES, EDWARD RILEY – CONNECTICUT, USA.

Established in 1868, the firm moved to Bridgeport in 1870 and became known as Ives & Blakeslee in 1872. The maker of good quality trains, metal toys, automata figures and walking toys, the company was taken over by Lionel in the late 1920s.

LAMBERT, LEOPOLD – PARIS.

Lambert originally worked for Vichy, and his automata are often identified with the mark 'L.B.' on their keys.

LEHMANN – BRANDENBURG, GERMANY.

The firm, founded in 1881, originally made cans and containers, before branching into novelty tinplate toys, which are always clearly marked. Johann Richter joined the firm in 1911. The company was sequestered by the Russians in 1949, but was re-established in Nuremberg in 1951 and is still in production today.

LESCHOT, JEAN FRÉDÉRIC – SWITZERLAND.

Leschot (1746-1827) worked on automata with Pierre Jaquet Droz.

LINEOL – BRANDENBURG, GERMANY.

The firm produced tinplate toys between 1934 and 1945, when it closed down.

LIONEL – NEW YORK, USA.

The firm was founded by Joshua Lionel Cowen (1881-1965) and specialized in trains. In 1901 it began trading as the Lionel Manufacturing Company and was part of the group to buy out Ives. The company was in decline after 1937 and was taken over by the Gilbert Cohn group.

LUCOTTE – PARIS.

Established c1795, little is known of the origins of this firm. Producing solid soliders and figures, it was taken over by Mignot.

LUTZ, LUDWIG – ELLWANGEN, GERMANY.

Trading between 1846 and 1891, the firm made tin toys and became known as Englert & Lutz after 1857. Bing also distributed Lutz products. The company finally sold out to Märklin.

MÄRKLIN – WÜRTTEMBERG, GERMANY.

Established in 1859, the firm traded as W. Märklin until 1888, when Gebrüder Märklin was set up. The name changed again in 1892 to Gebrüder Märklin & Co., and again in 1907 to Gebrüder Märklin & Cie. In 1922 the suffix 'GmbH' was added. The makers of fine quality tin toys, the firm is still in production.

MARTIN, FERNAND – PARIS.

The Paris factory was in production by 1880, specializing in tinplate toys which were often costumed in fabric and marked 'F.M.'. The firm continued in the 1920s under Victor Bonnet et Cie.

MARX, LOUIS – USA.

Born in 1894, in 1920 Marx took over the Strauss firm he had joined as an office boy. His company specialized in novelty toys and was the largest manufacturer in the world by the mid 1920s. Plastic toys were mainly produced after 1950.

METTOY – NORTHAMPTON, ENGLAND.

Founded in 1933 by Henry Ullman, the former proprietor of Tipp & Co., the company produced tinplate toys in the 1930s and '40s and marketed Corgi toys in the 1960s.

MIGNOT – PARIS.

Founded c1825, the firm began producing soldiers in 1838 when they began to use the mark 'C.B.G.', composed of the initials of the founders (Cuperly, Blondel and Gerbeau). The firm underwent several amalgamations, and Lucotte was incorporated after which his mark 'L.C.' with the Imperial bee is found on some work. The company is still in production.

MOKO – FÜRTH, GERMANY.

The trade name of Moses Kohnstam, the maker of tin toys, established c1875.

PHALIBOIS, J. – PARIS.

A maker of automata during the mid to late 19th century, Phalibois is especially known for his monkey figures, and his work is occassionally marked 'J.P.'.

PLANCK, ERNST – NUREMBERG, GERMANY.

Originally an instrument making company founded in 1866, it began to make electric railways in 1882, together with steam toys. Production ceased in the 1930s.

RADIGUET, M. – PARIS.

Producing steam engines from 1872, the firm is thought to have made its first steam trains in the 1880s. A partnership with Massiot was formed in 1889.

ROCK & GRANER – BIBERACH, GERMANY.

Established in 1813, by 1851 the firm was probably the largest maker of tin toys, although a slow decline in importance was seen after 1860. The maker of scenes, dolls' furniture and carriages, the firm became known as Rock & Graner Nachfolger (R. & G.N.) from 1896 to 1904 when the company was dissolved.

ROSSIGNOL – PARIS.

Founded in 1868, the firm made tin toys, often marked 'C.R.', and is thought to have made the first toy motor cars. The firm traded until 1962.

SCHOENNER, JEAN – NUREMBERG, GERMANY.

Founded in 1875, the company is best known for its larger-scale, steam-powered trains and boats. It ceased production in c1904.

SCHUCO – NUREMBERG, GERMANY.

Founded in 1912 by Schreyer & Muller, the firm made a wide assortment of novelty toys and plush-covered metal toys were introduced in 1920. The firm is still in production.

STEVENS MODEL DOCKYARD – LONDON.

Founded in 1843, the firm produced brass locomotives until 1912.

STOCK – SOLIGEN, GERMANY.

Founded in 1905 by Walter Stock, the firm made tinplate toys until ceasing production in the 1930s.

SUTCLIFFE – LEEDS, ENGLAND.

Founded by J.W. Sutcliffe in 1885, the firm made tinplate toys, specializing in boats of all kinds. Production ceased in 1984.

THÉROUDE, ALEXANDRE NICHOLAS – PARIS.

Théroude produced automata and toys from 1859, using the mark 'A.N. Théroude, Paris'.

TIPP & CO. – NUREMBERG, GERMANY.

Founded in 1912, the firm specialized in tin and military toys.

TRIANG – ENGLAND.

Founded in 1919 as an offshoot of the Lines family business by William, Arthur and Walter Lines, the first catalogue was issued in 1921 showing their wide variety of wood and metal toys. The brand name is again in use.

TOOTSIETOY – CHICAGO, USA.

A range of metal toys, especially dolls'-house furniture, made by the Dowst Manufacturing Co. Also one of the first makers of die-cast toys c1910.

UEBERLACKER – NUREMBERG, GERMANY.

Founded by Leonard Ueberlacker in 1871, the firm specialized in tinplate air and water toys.

VAUCANSON, JACQUES DE – GRENOBLE, FRANCE.

Vaucanson (1709-1782) was the maker of some spectacular automata which he exhibited at fairs. He eventually sold his work in 1743.

WELLS – LONDON.

Begun by A.W. Wells and registered in 1923, the company was a leading producer of lithographed tinplate until the late 1950s. The firm took over Brimtoy in 1932.

INDEX

ACKNOWLEDGEMENTS

Key: *t*=top; *b*=bottom; *l*=left; *r*=right; *i*=inset.

AUTHOR'S COLLECTION: pages 21, 41, 69 *b*, 100, 103, 105 *b*,
111 *t b*, 120 *tl tr*. B.K.L. DEVELOPMENTS LTD: page 118 *br*.
CHRISTIES EAST, NEW YORK; pages 110 *t b*. CHRISTIES, SOUTH
KENSINGTON: pages 6, 7, 8, 9, 45, 49, 51 *t b*, 53 *i*, 55 *l*, 58, 60
t b, 63 *l*, 65, 68, 71 *l*, 76/77, 82, 83, 84/5, 88, 90, 90/91,
101, 102/3, 106/7, 110 *l*, 113 *l*, 114, 118 *l*, 121. THE LOST
STREET MUSEUM, ROSS-ON-WYE: pages 44 *l*, 47 *b*, 48 *b*, 56, 59
l, 63 *b*, 66, 67 *l*, 69 *l*, 70 *l*, 70/71, 72, 73 *b*, 75, 77 *i*, 78 *l*, 78
b, 79, 80, 86, 89 *t b*, 92/93, 93, 94, 95, 96, 97, 98, 99. PHIL-
LIPS, LONDON: page 18. SOTHEBY'S, BILLINGHURST: pages 104,
106 *b*, 107 *l*, 115, 117, 122, 123. SOTHEBY'S, CHESTER: pages
118 *tr*, 119 *l* SOTHEBY'S, LONDON: pages 10 *l* 10/11, 13, 15 *lr*;
16 *lr*, 19 *l* 22 *lr*, 26, 27 *t b*, 28 *t b*, 29, 30, 31 *lr*, 32 *t b*, 33, 34,
35, 36, 37 *l*, 38 *lr*, 39, 43, 44 *b*, 46, 47, *l* 48 *l* 50 *t b*, 54, 55
b, 57 *b*, 59 *b*, 61, 62, 81 *t b*. SOTHEBY'S, NEW YORK: pages 12,
17, 19 *r*; 20, 23, 24, 25, 52/53. JANE VANDELL PICTURE LIB-
RARY: pages 14, 37 *r*; 40, 57 *l*, 64, 67 *b*, 73 *l*, 74, 87, 102,
105 *l*, 108, 109 *t b*, 112, 113 *b*, 116, 119 *b*, 120 *b*.